Around the World in 349 Days

# Around the World in 349 Days

## A Diary 1975

Jeff Harrison

Copyright © 2023 Jeff Harrison
All rights reserved.
ISBN: 9780645715316

## Contents

| | |
|---|---|
| Maps | i |
| Introduction – A Wider Horizon | v |
| Part I – Hello World | 1 |
|     Buying equipment to 'hit the road' | 20 |
|     Hitchhiking in Europe in the 1970s | 23 |
|     One with the wind in a Citroen 2CV | 63 |
| Part II – Summer Days as a Swaggie | 88 |
|     Losing my opal dress ring in Tiaret, Algeria | 96 |
|     Breaking the egg | 107 |
|     My moment on top of the mountain | 139 |
| Part III – Downhill to Home | 180 |
|     A night in hospital in Kabul | 188 |
|     My 'smack' surprise | 204 |
| Epilogue – A Transformation | 226 |
| Glossary | 229 |
| Author Bio | 231 |

\* There is a colour edition of this book (ISBN: 9780645715309) with a slightly larger format (17.8 x 25.4 cm).

# MAPS

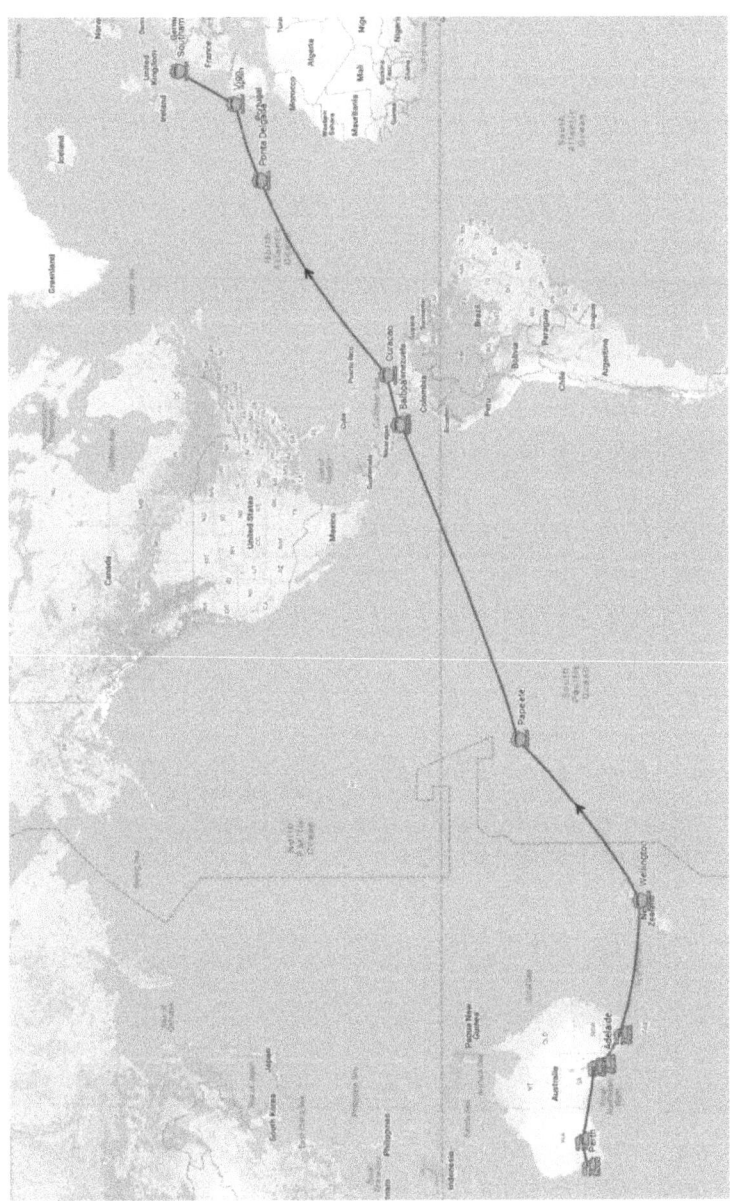

Map 1: Perth, Western Australia to Melbourne, Victoria on the Trans Australian Railway.  Melbourne to Southampton, UK on the S.S. Ellinis
17 JAN 1975 to 27 FEB 1975

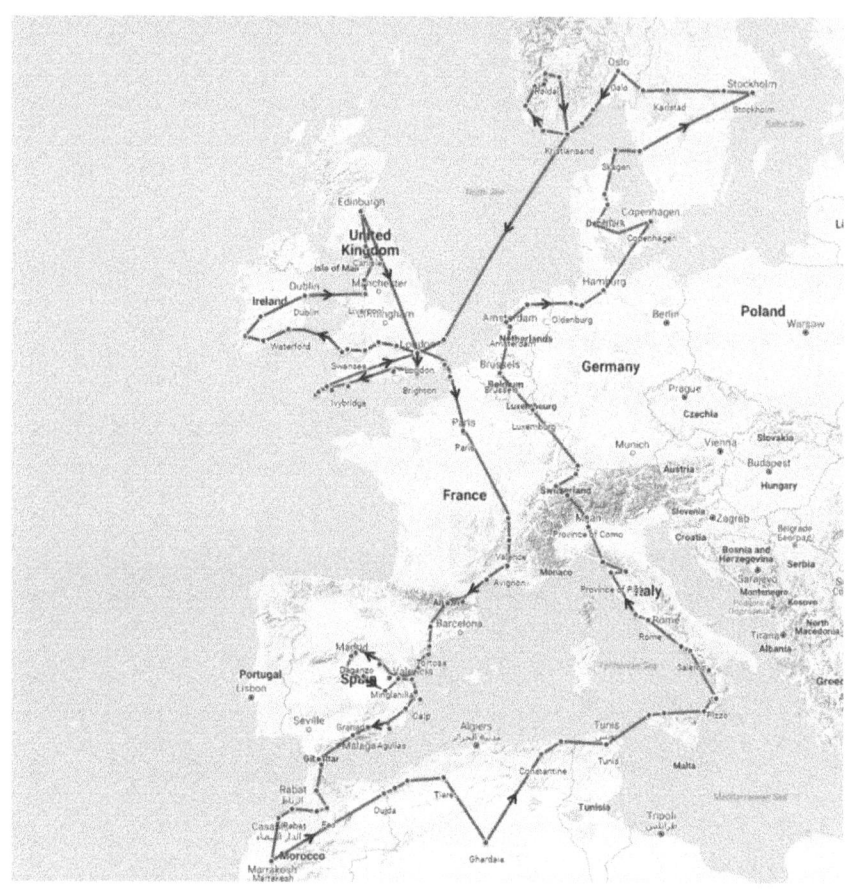

Map 2: London, Europe, North Africa, Europe, London
28 FEB 1975 to 28 AUG 1975

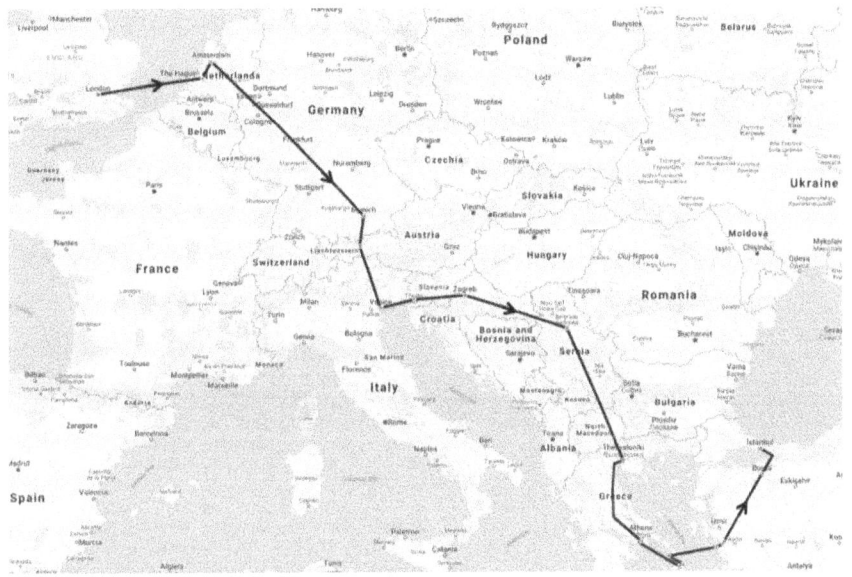

Map 3: London to Istanbul
29 AUG 1975 to 30 SEP 1975

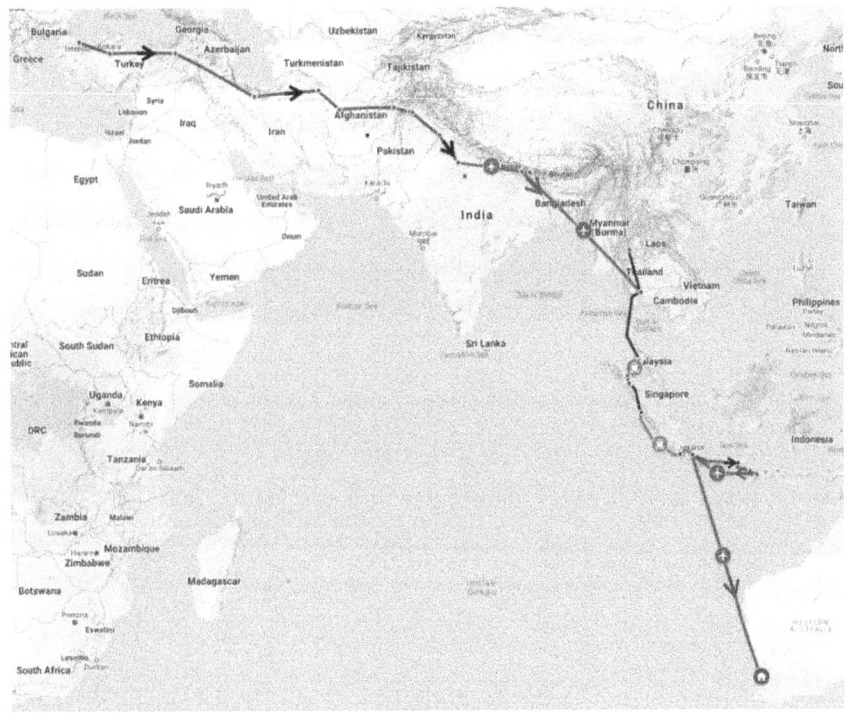

Map 4: Istanbul to Perth (including the Magic Bus)
1 OCT 1975 to 1 JAN 1976

## INTRODUCTION – A WIDER HORIZON

Early in the second half of 1974, my friend John – at twenty-two, a year older than me – asked me to go with him to check out the Greek passenger ship S.S. Patris while it was berthed at Fremantle, Western Australia. It was en route to Melbourne and then across the Pacific and North Atlantic, via the Panama Canal, to Southampton in the UK.

In those days it was a rite of passage for young adult Australians to 'do the overland'. That usually meant a ticket to Europe, hitchhiking around for a few months, perhaps crossing into North Africa, and then return to Australia along a trans-Asian route from Turkey, through South Asia and Southeast Asia.

John's and my home city of Perth is the world's most isolated capital. We keenly felt that isolation as young men whose teenage years were on the periphery of the wakening 'Flower Power' hippie counterculture of the 1960s. Except for a few hundred kilometres due south, we could travel three thousand kilometres along the other points of the compass before we'd find anything more than seawater, desert, or despair.

As products of the Australian education system and cultural mores of the 1950s through to the early 1970s, we were primarily children of the old British Empire. The world maps on our classroom walls were dominated by pink coloured countries representing the Commonwealth of Nations. We were taught a history that was more British than Australian and, consequently, many of us were keen to journey to Europe and see our 'history' for ourselves.

So, John easily persuaded me to join him on an overseas trip. By December I had left my public service office job, sold my car and stereo, collected my passport, booked my passage Perth to Melbourne on the Trans-Australian Railway, and bought a one-way ticket on the S.S. Patris's sister ship S.S. Ellinis, departing from Port Melbourne on 25<sup>th</sup> January for Southampton UK. In 1975 it was less expensive to travel to Europe by ship than to fly.

I was off to see the world. I had a small suitcase and about fifteen hundred Australian dollars' worth of Thomas

Cook traveller's cheques. German deutschmarks were the favoured travel currency then and I had two booklets of them – a few fifty DM cheques, but mostly one hundred DM. I calculated, if I cashed a hundred DM (around thirty Australian dollars) a week, I could travel for about a year.

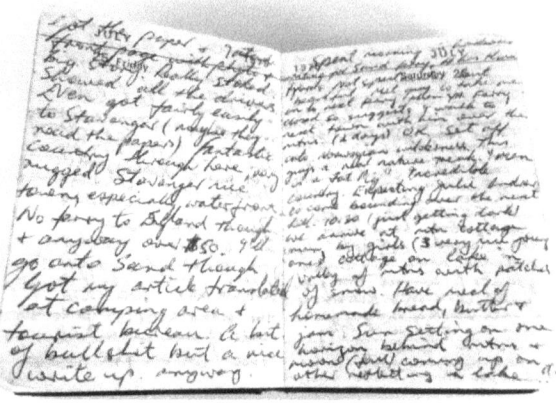

## Collins Diary 1975

I wanted to record my overseas adventure. It was decades before digital photography, and longer before smartphones, so I took a pocket Collins Diary 1975 – 9cm by 7cm and one day to a page. The following text in Segoe Print font is transcribed from my pocket diary. Sometimes I'd catch up with an entry a day or two after the event so, a few times, the chronological flow might be inconsistent.

Occasionally I'd enter a 'Diary Note' in the few pages provided at the end of the diary. For continuity I've included them into the appropriate diary page transcription.

I've also added occasional afterward explanatory notes where they seemed useful.

## Letters, postcards, and snippets

Sometimes I'd send a letter or a postcard home to my parents in Perth. They are transcribed in Segoe Script font.

Not carrying a camera, I would collect free tourist bureau brochures and tear out snippets of photos of places I'd visited. I'd write brief explanatory comments on them and include them in my letters – Mum & Dad kept them all. I've annotated some of the snippets with those contemporaneous comments.

I also carried a small notepad and used it to jot down useful info, calculate currency conversions, make destination signs for hitchhiking, and occasionally, record some impressions or scribble a time-filling whimsy. I've used Segoe Script to reproduce some of those scribblings.

## Part I – Hello World

When I decided to head off and 'see the world' I was a callow twenty-one-year-old; the only son, and middle child, of a middle-class suburban family. I was employed in a dull job, at which I performed satisfactorily, and on weekends I surfed, I listened to rock 'n' roll, and I partied. During my final year of primary school and first year of high school my family lived in Adelaide, South Australia but, otherwise, I hadn't been outside of Western Australia. Except for the local Italian greengrocer, I had scant exposure to non-Anglo-Saxon cultures.

As was common among my friends, I found a job shortly after I'd completed high school, and I'd moved out of my parents' home several months before my eighteenth birthday. It was typical to live in a share house of about half a dozen similarly aged co-tenants – mostly male. My core group of friends were all generally late starters in the girlfriend stakes. 'Relationships' were often brief encounters, and commonly initiated at drunken parties or pub sessions. I was mostly pessimistic when it came to girls because I was a physically small person – below average height and slim build. My friend John was an amiable six-foot-plus gentle giant. Mum's anxiety about my intention to travel overseas was mitigated when she learnt I would be traveling with him.

My Australian passport photo was taken in late 1974. It's a picture of me as a nine-to-five, Monday-to-Friday, government office worker. I can remember the typical 'disco' style of clothes I was wearing at the time: high-waisted cardigans; rounded shirt collars; and beltless flared slacks. Friday nights were for going to a pub to listen to a favourite rock band while drinking to excess or, if we were lucky, there might have been a party somewhere. Saturdays were for surfing and hangover recovery, Sundays were for mucking about with friends, listening to LP records, or backyard cricket, and ending with the afternoon session at the local pub.

So, John and I headed off on our adventure; innocent, wide-eyed, and open to experience whatever we may discover. After we sailed from Port Melbourne on the S.S. Ellinis we were onboard the ship for just over four and a half weeks before we would disembark at Southampton in the UK. Our fellow passengers were mostly mature ex-pats returning to Europe, but there were some younger travelling types either going home after exploring the Antipodes or heading off for Europe and beyond – like John and myself. Between ports there was not a lot for us youthful and predominately male passengers to do but enjoy the duty-free alcohol, smoke marijuana (either smuggled on board or purchased at ports en route), and party together as we discussed future travel plans. Then we arrived in London.

The first week we explored central London. Over the following several weeks John and I travelled through South West England together; we crossed the Channel to France where we split up; then I continued by myself through Spain and across North-West Africa. I acquired basic hitchhiking skills, and I began to develop an appreciation and enjoyment of the exotica of foreign countries and cultures, but I was also somewhat shocked when I arrived in Morocco and first experienced travelling within a non-Western country.

More temperate readers of my diary may be a little shocked (or dismayed) at my younger-self's enthusiasm for alcohol and recreational drugs. I offer the following by way of explanation, but not as an excuse, or with any regrets.

My parents were 1960s party people: barbecues and beer; dancing The Twist; sparkling wine; fashionable cigarettes. Through my childhood and formative years social imbibing of alcohol seemed commonplace, widely promoted, and effectively socially obligatory. The negative-health effects of alcohol, and cigarettes, were not widely acknowledged or discussed. I learnt party-time drinking from watching my ebullient parents and their friends and family – since my early teens I was drinking at parties. By my late teens drinking to get drunk was normal and acceptable behaviour among my peers. Sometime someone introduced us to marijuana, which we thoroughly enjoyed – I remember a lot of laughter, and

*My parents on their "first dirty weekend away", as Mum described it. A photo from probably about the late 1940s.*

munchies. When I partied, I was invariably a happy drunk. The effect alcohol and marijuana had on my perceptions and mood amused me, and I enjoyed the consequent uninhibitedness.

Since my middle high school years, I was an avid reader, and I most enjoyed books that were a bit subversive. J D Salinger's 'The Catcher in the Rye' was included in our school curriculum. My keen response to it prompted our English teacher to lend me her 'Catch 22' by Joseph Heller. I also discovered Kurt Vonnegut and J.P. Donleavy. At about age twenty I was astounded by Albert Camus's 'The Outsider' which introduced me to his philosophy of absurdism. All these authors, I suppose, influenced my developing attitudes, and could be categorised as being rebellious or, at least, nonconformist.

Maybe inebriation suited that idea of being a bit of a rebel; maybe it also suited my emerging personal sense of absurdism. Anyway, I didn't drink alone, almost everybody I met up with along the way was drinking too, and we had a lot of fun.

## Perth to Melbourne

**17 JAN 1975**

We left the station 9:30PM and spent the night in the bar. We staggered back to our cabin with three new friends. I tried to boof a Darwin refugee.

During Christmas 1974 the Northern Territory capital Darwin was devastated by Tropical Cyclone Tracy. Evacuees were relocated across Australia.

**18 JAN 1975**

The two refugee chicks got off in Kalgoorlie – bummer.

Kalgoorlie is a mid-sized mining town and the train's first stop; about 600 km east of Perth.

We were too hungover to go to the bar, so we stayed in the cabin and John went "berserk".

John had difficulty coping with the oppressive confines of our small cabin and the relentless nothingness of the vast Nullarbor Plain we were traversing; he joked about going "berserk".

At dinner the apple sauce with the pork was the leftover compote of fruit from breakfast. We're going to the bar at 8PM. I don't think anything else will happen.

**19 JAN 1975**

Nothing happened on the Trans-Aust.

The Trans Australian Railway is the rail link between Western Australia and the eastern states of Australia. The passenger service we were on is better known as the Indian Pacific.

> We switched trains at Port Pirie, had two hours in Adelaide, then we sat up for fourteen hours to Melbourne. We drank cans of beer and Canadian Club on the train but had to pack it in at 2AM because people were complaining.

**20 JAN 1975 to 24 JAN 1975**

We stayed at John's cousin's place in Melbourne while we waited a few days until our scheduled departure on the S.S. Ellinis. We explored a bit of the city, mostly the pubs, and a little of the near coast. A few selected diary entries provide an outline.

> Arrived in Melbourne. It looked shitty at first impression. Still, it's nice in places. Molly's house is unreal. We saw JO'K at the Armidale pub.

Molly Meldrum was the host of the nation's most influential TV pop-music show 'Countdown'. Johnny O'Keefe was an iconic 1950s style Australian rock 'n' roller.

> The barman is giving us an address in France.
>
> The radio station 3XY is unreal.
>
> Toorak where the millionaires live...really big old mansions. They really know what houses are all about in Melbourne. New houses look out of place.
>
> We took a drive down the coast to Mornington. A surprisingly beautiful coast with picturesque bays.

## Melbourne to Southampton (aboard the S.S. Ellinis)

**25 JAN 1975**

*We left Port Melbourne at 10PM with nobody to see us off. Our 4-berth cabin is on 'C' deck, room 608, second bottom deck right up front. It's fairly neat. It's a nicer boat than the Patris.*

Our cabin was modest, cramped and no bathroom, but the ship's common facilities were very good. Meals were included, the plentiful entertainment was free, and alcohol and tobacco were duty free. My one-way fare Melbourne to Southampton cost a little over AUD300.

**22/01/1975**
**Letter on the back of the S.S. Ellinis mailing list**

*Dear Mum and Dad,*
*I thought you may need this mailing list in case you want to get in touch with me while I'm on the boat. The train trip wasn't as good as we expected. The first night was good but we were sick the next day and didn't really recover until we got to Melbourne. Still, we met a good crowd and had a lot of fun at times.*
*We had to sit up for 14 hours from Adelaide to Melbourne. I'm just starting to get into this travelling thing. It's great carrying everything you own in one small suitcase – really 'free as the breeze'. Should be even better when we get going. Anyway, I'm out of paper, I'll send you a postcard from somewhere.*
*Love Jeff*

From **25 JAN 1975 to 27FEB 1975** we were on the ship for thirty-two nights. Because my diary entries between ports became repetitive (as were the days), I've grouped some of those days' entries and selected a few sentences to, hopefully, provide a sketch.

**26 JAN 1975 to 28 JAN 1975**

*The first night in bed was claustrophobic. Meals are good. No chicks. We met some Pommies, Keith and Bob, and we played monopoly and got pissed – a good afternoon. Pissed as a fart* at dinner. We upset the posh people from Kew, and the Spanish chick.

We had designated table seating for meals. There was an older UK couple from Kew and a thirty-something Spanish lady, all conservatively mannered and understandably unimpressed with my, and John's, drunkenness at the table.

I didn't get up till 12 o'clock. I forgot to reset my watch and missed breakfast and lunch.

Sailing east we passed through several time zones and the onboard time would change periodically.

We reached New Zealand. Freaky lights on the water look like navigation lights. Wellington in the morning.

**29 JAN 1975**

Wellington is beautiful and very mountainous. Three of us hired a Mini and we toured Wellington. Milk is 4c a bottle, with a 9c deposit. A 35oz jug of beer is 48c. There's forest everywhere, and houses are built on cliffs – an isolated city and unspoiled. The navigation lights last night were Japanese fishing boats.

**29/01/1975**
**Postcard from Wellington, New Zealand**

## Melbourne to Southampton (aboard the S.S. Ellinis)

> Hi,
> just got into Wellington harbour. It looks really beautiful. Everything is built up onto cliffs, all pine forest and mountains.
> Seeya, Love Jeff

### 30 JAN 1975 to 2 FEB 1975

> We crossed the International Date Line. Watched a cabaret — great stuff! I caught the flu! Incredible, in the middle of the bloody Pacific and I get the flu! I started playing in a chess tournament — I'm coming second.

Board games were popular in the days before home computer games and smartphones. The complex table-top fantasy game of 'Dungeons & Dragons' was gaining a devoted following after the widespread literary triumphs of J.R.R. Tolkien's 'The Hobbit' and 'Lord of the Rings'. But chess was favoured in my circle of friends. It was portable and much simpler to set up with concise rules, yet it was infinitely complex, and it provided the one-on-one competition we wanted as male youths. Throughout my yearlong travels I was happy to discover it was widely played — beginning on the ship. Chess may have been internationally popular at the time owing to the recent phenomena of America's Bobby Fischer and his successful, and newsworthy, 1972 World Championship match with Boris Spassky of the Soviet Union.

> I'm going to bed early to try and lose this flu. I've forgotten most of today. I think I gave the flu to John. I slept outside and woke up about 3 o'clock. I had a smoke with some deadshits ("hey man" every 2 seconds). Tahiti was visible at 4 o'clock, then I fell asleep.

### 3 FEB 1975

> Tahiti is magnificent! It's everything they say it is. It's not very commercial on the far side. Me and John, and two others, hired a car and explored. We bathed under a waterfall — unreal, just like the movies. The car blew up and we hitched a ride back with two French chicks. We had lunch in a little bar

Melbourne to Southampton (aboard the S.S. Ellinis)

*– we had to point to what we wanted. Everything is VERY expensive. We had an unreal time – the best yet.*

**4 FEB 1975 to 13 FEB 1975**

*I woke late, and then started drinking and playing cards with Ken, Tom and John.*

Ken was a fellow Australian also heading for travelling adventures in Europe. He was an amiable, solid built character who was on his own and joined the kernel of our little onboard social group. Tom was a seasoned American traveller; a few years older than us and handsomely moustachioed. He had passage to Cristobal where he was disembarking to explore South America.

*Woke late as usual with a big hangover. No smoking or drinking today – I took it easy.*
*Went to a movie. The same old routine day.*
*There was a fancy dress ball. English beer is a good drop.*
*We got into smoking with Tom and Jeannie (also Martyn). We'd usually meet in a cabin after tea, then up to the disco, then either the Outrigger Bar or bed.*

Jeannie was petite and pretty with a short bob of auburn hair and long eyelashes. She was escaping waitressing in Sydney and always seemed cheerful. She and Tom had hooked up soon after we boarded ship in Melbourne and theirs and our partying interests often coincided. Martyn was an English passenger, about our age, with below shoulder-length flowing black locks and, to our unworldly minds, he seemed to be a bit 'posh'.

*I got ripped with Jeannie, Tom, and Martyn. The corridors and stairs are the test.*

It was a challenge when stoned to negotiate the narrow corridors along the cabin decks, and the occasional narrow spiral stairways between decks, especially while the ship was being buffeted by high seas.

*... we went to a clown show – not bad (there was a 62-year-old tap dancer). Got ripped again (again) then to the Outrigger*

Bar with Tom and Jeannie. We stayed up till 2:30AM before bed.

**05/02/1975 & 13/02/1975**
**Two postcards from S.S. Ellinis (somewhere east of Panama)**

Hi, we got into Tahiti early on Monday 3rd. That place is magnificent. This postcard doesn't do the country justice. Pape'ette wasn't much but still a lot less commercial than I thought. We hired a car and circumnavigated the island (it's only 90 miles around).

Sometimes my descriptions alternated between imperial and metric measurements (also in my diary). My generation was mostly educated in imperial, but metrication in Australia occurred slowly through the 1970s, hence my use of both systems.

The island is just a huge mountain range sticking out of the ocean. There are no roads across the island — just around. Jungle everywhere full of coconuts, breadfruit etc. We even hiked through some jungle to get to a waterfall about 150 — 200 feet high and stripped off and had a shower just like in the movies. Stinking hot sitting under beautiful freshwater falling from a 200-foot cliff with coconut palms, butterflies, climbing ivy, wild hibiscus all around — fantastic —

## Melbourne to Southampton (aboard the S.S. Ellinis)

everything I expected the South Pacific to be. So much more to say but no room. I got another postcard...

*Our cabin*

(13/02/75)

I didn't buy any presents in Tahiti because everything was incredibly expensive. We get to the Panama Canal at 5AM tomorrow. We stop at Curacao, so I'll try there. Ship-life is very lazy. Food is great, cabin is pretty good, nightlife is entertaining. Beer is cheap (22 cents a can) but usually warm, cigarettes 33 cents a pack. I'm having bad luck with jeans — lost one pair in the laundry and broke a zip in another — down to one pair — will have to buy some in Panama. I'm in a chess tournament and doing pretty well. I should finish in the top 3 out of 26 starters. Being on a ship is not a bad way to get somewhere. Even if you get bored it's a good way to get bored. It's going to be a big shock, I think, when we get off.

Seeya later

Love Jeff

**14 FEB 1975**

Woke up at 5:30AM — Panama!. Balboa looked like a big city. The Canal is nothing much except for locks. We arrived at

## Melbourne to Southampton (aboard the S.S. Ellinis)

Cristobal 3PM. We saw Tom off on the train then hit the town. Town was a real dump. Very Americanised – stars and stripes everywhere. The ghetto was insane – a gang fight in an alley. A taxi driver was after me. Things were still pretty expensive, but I bought some jeans. PS: Yanks in the Panama Canal Zone are everything Yanks are supposed to be, i.e. sunnies, baseball caps, guns – 'bigger 'n better'.

**15 FEB 1975**

I got very drunk for the hell of it. I had a good time I think – I don't remember much.

**16 FEB 1975**

Curacao is very touristy.

Curacao is a Caribbean Island off the north coast of Venezuela and was a port of call; it was part of the Netherlands Antilles.

Black guys were offering dope in the streets. There's a casino – big money won and lost by the ship's crew. We hitched a ride without even trying. We were just standing on the roadside, ready to go back to the ship, when a beautiful chick stopped and gave us a lift.

## Melbourne to Southampton (aboard the S.S. Ellinis)

**Postcard of Curacao**

*Curacao is built right on the ocean inside the remains of an old fort. The town is spotless (for tourism) and all the original buildings are done up. The harbour is about 3 km inland and the pontoon bridge is floating on about 20 boat hulls so that when a ship has to go through, they just swing the bridge away. The casino is on the ground floor of a big new building. It's the only modern building we saw. The whole place is an island (I forgot how big but I'd say it's pretty big — about Kangaroo Island size).*

Kangaroo Island is off the South Australian coast and Curacao is about a tenth its size.

*Everyone runs around in huge American cars. Everybody is black and friendly.*

**17 FEB 1975 to 22 FEB 1975**

*I played for the chess tournament title — I won! I'm not the best player on the boat (Martyn is), but he lost one and drew one when I only lost one (to Martyn).*

Martyn was a very good chess player. He amazed me by occasionally playing blind-folded and, one time, we broke from a blind-fold game for lunch; then we continued with the game afterwards. He won without looking at the board to familiarise himself with the game position before resuming.

>...went to a folk and pop concert – it was pretty good.
>
>I'm reading a lot of books.
>
>Jeannie says we're touring England with her, and Ken will join us?!

**19/02/1975**
**Letter on 'Blue Sea Cruises by Chandris Lines' notepaper**

>Hi!
>
>Thought I'd write a letter to fill you in on the details that I've left out in the postcards, also to tell you about Panama and Cristobal and Curacao. To start with I forgot to tell you that the car we hired in Tahiti was a left-hand drive (they all are) and driving on the right-hand side is very strange but a lot of fun. John started driving and, in a few streets, ended up on the wrong side of the road (I just kept reaching for the door handle to change gears). Also, the chess tournament on the boat that I was in – I won it!!! (no prize yet though).
>
>I forgot if I wrote to you about Panama Canal but, in case I didn't, the canal itself wasn't much, just a river with jungle on the side and American flags everywhere. But the locks were fascinating – the leaflet tells you all about them. Christabel was an education. The first real slums I've seen – they were just like the movies too. Gang fights, drunks, pros – the works. Curacao was beautiful. It's a real tourist place. Very clean with a casino and a huge five-star pub. The whole population was cool black guys – also just like the movies. They all wore crazy clothes (yellow shirts, purple pants, red hats, bells, bangles, rhythm). The casino was really something. All the crew members really betted up big, cashing hundred-dollar bills. One guy dropped $1,000 on the night. Another guy won $500 on one go on the poker machines. I lost $0.75 and drank a lot of free drinks.

Melbourne to Southampton (aboard the S.S. Ellinis)

So far, all the so-called duty-free ports have been the most expensive. Prices in Curacao were higher than Perth. I think I'll do my shopping in Europe. I'm told it's cheaper. I think I'll send the suitcase back. There's a girl at our dinner table who's Spanish and me and John are learning a few words. I'd really like to pick up a few foreign languages. Nothing much else except I got diarrhoea like half the rest of the boat. The weather's getting colder. I'm learning to play bridge and I don't miss working in the least.

Buenas noches,

love Jeff.

**23 FEB 1975**

Arrived at Azores. A great place – very old.

The Azores is an archipelago in the mid-Atlantic and is an autonomous region of Portugal. The capital, Ponta Delgada, was a port of call.

We went to a marketplace and found Miguel's Bar with home grown wine with no additives. Three 10 oz glasses and you get blotto. Me, John, Bazza, Terry, Ken and Greg bought $26 worth in a huge bottle inside a woven cane cover. Us and another bunch were pissed and carrying bottles of wine back to the ship through the streets and singing. Six others bought in and we knocked it all off that arvo. And no hangover in the morning.

Melbourne to Southampton (aboard the S.S. Ellinis)

**24/02/1975**
**Letter on notepad paper added to the letter of 19/02/1975**

Hi again!

I couldn't send a letter at Ponta Delgada because they ran out of stamps on board and the post offices were shut (Sunday). Ponta Delgada was fabulous. It was our first taste of Europe. All the roads were cobblestone, and the buildings were ancient and small and damp. People just stared at us, and all the kids followed us around. First we just walked around looking at the sights.

About a mile out of town it became little farms with stone walls and cobblestones everywhere. Being Sunday, all the locals were in these little old churches everywhere with bells chiming away. We went into a huge mansion (a big white government house on a hill with swimming pool and private pine forest, huge gardens, a few acres of hay in the front, statues, etc.) It was the only sign of wealth we saw. Sort of like the local land baron. Then we went back into town past the marketplace. Just like you would imagine, it sold everything from toys to eels. Also, you buy live rabbits or ducks for eating.

We met up with a couple of people from the boat and went to a tiny bar up one of the streets. The bar was just one room that opened onto the street. It had three stools in it and all he sold was beer or wine. The wine was incredible. He made it himself and it was just pure grape. The first glass was okay but the second knocked you. After the third you were screaming. There were about 20 of us in the bar toward the end. The owner was terrific. He spoke little English and prided himself on his honesty and his wine. He gave out free goat cheese (also made himself) but you had to take it in your mouth off his great bloody big carving knife which he held out. He also gave out free fish and bananas.

We ended up buying 800 ounces of wine in a huge bottle shaped like this. We took it in

## Melbourne to Southampton (aboard the S.S. Ellinis)

turns of carrying it to the boat (two guys at a time), it was damn heavy. We knocked it off that afternoon between 12 of us – we all got pretty drunk. But, as the barman said, nobody got a hangover. By the way, buenas noches means good night so adios,

Love Jeff.

*This town is all we saw*
*Nice Town. The bar was up there →*

**24 FEB 1975 to 25 FEB 1975**

Arrived in Vigo, Spain. We got pretty drunk with Keith and John drinking sangria in a little back-alley bar

**26 FEB 1975**

The last night on board so there were parties all over the boat. The ship's crew got heavy – there were a few fights. We smoked and drank all night with Bazza and Terry.

Bazza and Terry were returning home to England after touring around Australia for a year. When the ship cabins were allocated during boarding in Melbourne, they were lucky enough to win a suite above deck. They shared it with four other passengers with bunk beds added in the cabin lounge area. It was the pick of the cabins for our parties; it even had big square windows with views of the ocean.

It may have been their excitement to be returning home after many months away, and perhaps combined with their sometimes derision of non-Anglos, but Bazza and Terry partied especially hard and would often rankle the Greek crew.

Then we snuck into the ship kitchen with the munchies. We found some trays of roast chickens, but we got chased out. I woke up Jeannie and took her back to our cabin for a boof.

**27 FEB 1975**

Arrived in Southampton. A very cold but sunny day.

Bazza and Terry's boisterous behaviour was even less appreciated when they 'celebrated' by throwing some of their cabin furniture and accessories through the big windows onto the Southampton dock below.

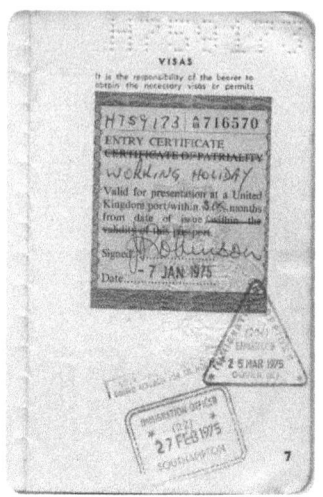

Customs was not as bad as I'd imagined. We caught a Walkabout bus to London and stayed at the club. It was very expensive.

The Walkabout Club in the 1970s provided short-term accommodation in London, travel information and services, and was a general meeting place. It catered primarily for travellers from Australia and New Zealand.

**28 FEB 1975 to 1 MAR 1975**

John, Ken, and me and Jeannie got a room in Kensington between us for £8.50 a week each.

Impressions of London. Pretty exciting at first – hard to realise I'm actually here. I didn't think it was as big as I'd imagined it would be after seeing Trafalgar and Piccadilly etc. But when you realise that it's like that all over, then you know it's very big. Also very crowded, old, dirty, and expensive.

**2 MAR 1975 to 5 MAR 1975**

I keep spending £1 as if its $1. I don't like cab drivers. The underground becomes boring after a while, buses are better (2 storey). The 'name' sights (e.g. Buckingham Palace) are disappointing except for Big Ben and Hampton Court. There are pubs everywhere but not pubs as we know them. They're

> *more like little cafes.*

The trend in Perth in the 1970s, and through to the 1990s, was for pubs to be very big venues, usually with a music stage and several bars. The intimate atmosphere of the London pubs was a delightful new experience for us.

> *The beer is good but Watneys Red bitter gives you a hell of a hangover (22p a pint). It's not really warm but cool. You never see a drunk or even anybody getting loud. It's all very refined. Hyde Park Speaker's Corner is a joke. If it wasn't for the hecklers nobody would go. Wages are shocking (£30-40 per week) and prices are disgusting. A quote from a German traveller "around England there is an atmosphere of decadence, a feeling of a crumbling empire" – he's pretty well right.*

The UK had been in economic recession since 1973 and was suffering stagflation: high unemployment and inflation; hence my observation of London's low wages and high prices.

**6 MAR 1975 to 7 MAR 1975**

> *London is great for entertainment though there are very few big-name groups left. Live theatre is best. We saw 'John, Paul, George, Ringo and Bert'. It was really fantastic with John really exactly like John Lennon.*

'John, Paul, George, Ringo and Bert' was a musical about the Beatles that ran for a year at the Lyric theatre. It was The Evening Standard 'Best Musical of 1974' award winner.

> *Also saw 'Oh! Calcutta' – very shit-house, very dirty.*

'Oh! Calcutta' was an infamous theatrical review featuring sex-related sketches and a lot of nudity. I didn't find it especially amusing, except for the abundant and intentionally shocking display of genitalia.

> *I met Greg M\* and Kim P\*. They're both off to Majorca.*

Greg and Kim were local acquaintances from Perth. They were one or two years older than me. Majorca meant nothing to me then, and I don't know if it was a youthful clubbing mecca in those days. But Greg and

Kim were at the forefront of our socially cool; I can imagine they could have heard of, and been drawn to, any Majorcan party centre that may have existed then.

**8 MAR 1975 to 13 MAR 1975 – Blank Pages, a remembered summary:**

These pages in my diary are blank most likely because I was too busy exploring London to find time to write any entries.

John, Ken, Jeannie and I based ourselves at an inexpensive bedsit at Vicarage Gate, Kensington. Our room was cold, damp and dark. Jeannie and I had become an 'item' and, as befitted our age and the times, were sexually uninhibited – much to the annoyance of John who slept in the adjoining bed. Down an outside corridor was a bathroom we shared with the other lodgers. It had a gas meter at the doorway that had to be fed with coins for hot water. A rudimentary breakfast was included: white bread with fruitless strawberry jam, and weak tea. London in 1975 was still infamous for the blandness of its cuisine, and meals at cafés were variations of processed meats, eggs, baked beans, and chips. We supplemented our meals by purchasing some food; we discovered we could 'refrigerate' it by placing it on the outside windowsill.

We spent our days eagerly roaming London and recognising features we had learnt of in our largely British-focussed Australian education: The Underground was novel, useful, and challenging; the city architecture was a marvel; and the London pubs, with pints of cool dark ale and roast dinners, were a joy.

But after a while John and I were keen to head out into the world we'd come to see. Ken and Jeannie hadn't arrived with the same plans or resources as us. I was tempted to stay with Jeannie but organized to head off with John for an initial few days of hitchhiking around South West England and then back to London when Jeannie and I might consider our options.

## BUYING EQUIPMENT TO 'HIT THE ROAD'

I had travelled to the UK with just a small suitcase of clothes so I needed to equip myself with hitchhiking gear before we headed out on the road. London had a wider range of kit than was available in Australia, and cheaper prices. We found an army surplus and camping supply shop off Haymarket near Piccadilly Circus in central London; it could supply everything we needed.

The first necessary item was a backpack. The talk among intending hitchhikers on the S.S. Ellinis was about the new H-frame design. The old-style backpacks were formless bags with a couple of shoulder straps whereas the H-frames were an aluminium tube frame (unsurprisingly in an 'H' shape) with multi-pocketed nylon compartments attached. There were padded shoulder straps fixed to the frame and an additional waist-belt strap that took a lot of the weight off your shoulders. Another advantage was, when unharnessed, the backpack could be stood on the frame and leaned against something to stand upright and off the ground. Usually there was a space at the base of the frame to strap a sleeping bag or tent.

I chose a teal green nylon canvas backpack with a matching green aluminium H-frame. It was divided horizontally into two main compartments. The top was closed with a large weather-protecting over-flap, and the lower had a zippered opening. There were four smaller side pockets, and the weather flap had an extra outside flat Velcro pocket. There was space on the frame under the lower compartment to strap a rolled nylon sleeping bag. I dedicated the lower compartment to my limited selection of clothes. Into the top went my tent, any reserve food, a small ex-army water bottle, a book, and sundry items. There was also room for a Gaz Globetrotter cooker which was a brilliant combination of a burner unit, a replaceable gas bottle, and two small aluminium cooking pots. The bottle and burner cleverly packed away into the pots to create a space-saving 20 x 10 cm cylinder. Smaller sundries went into the backpack side pockets.

It was the fashion among hitchhikers to attach a small flag of their country of origin to the outside of the pack; I suppose to identify themselves to potential lifts. I couldn't find a suitable Australian flag, so I used an indelible white marker to draw a rough outline map of Australia on the outer over-flap. I don't recall anybody ever noticing it, let alone recognising what it represented.

My tent was primitive by modern standards. It was blue nylon, one person only, had wooden poles in two pieces that were joined by a metal socket, and it was flyless (there were several times when everything in the tent was soaked wet overnight). I bought a black, waist-length, water resistant, padded nylon jacket with several large pockets. I also bought a small ex-army map satchel. It was heavy canvas with a shoulder strap and had handy internal compartments. It kept my passport, traveller's cheques, diary, notebook, maps and pens.

My pride and joy was a pair of Czechoslovakian hiking boots. They were made from thick but soft leather, ankle-high, and had rugged rubber soles and, importantly, the uppers were a deep maroon colour, and the stitching and laces were contrasting golden yellow.

**14 MAR 1975**

*We're trying to get organised, me and John are leaving London tomorrow. I abandoned my suitcase and pyjamas – I left them to charity. I left Jeannie's stuff with Walkabout.*

Jeannie was away for a few days on a Walkabout skiing trip to Austria and had left a few things at our bedsit. She hadn't let us know what she wanted us to do with the few things she left behind. The best option we could find was to leave them at Walkabout and leave a message for her.

**15 MAR 1975**

*At last! We got a green bus out of London to Reigate then started hitching.*

The familiar red London buses serviced the metro areas. London's Green Line coaches serviced the outer regions.

*We got a lift straight off to Brighton. My pack is too heavy. Brighton is nicer than I expected. We met up with Pete and decided to camp out for the night. We had a few beers at a recreation centre.*

A feature of this style of travelling was continually meeting, and re-meeting, people travelling on a similar route. It was common to join up and briefly explore together; some liaisons lasted longer than others, and some I remember better. Unless there is a definitive explanation necessary to my story I haven't expanded on all the names I mention.

**16 MAR 1975**

*I woke up as cold as I've ever been. The windward side of my tent had iced up. I had no feeling in my feet or hands. I* showered and sat in a basin with my feet in hot water. I felt better. We walked out of Brighton. My shoulder was killing me. It took eight lifts to get to Southampton. We passed Polney on the way, it looked really nice. We'll stay in a hostel tonight.

**17 MAR 1975**

I sent some clothes back home to lighten my pack. We started hitching and we got to Totton, then got a bus out to Salisbury. It started to snow at Southampton! We got a lift to the main road. We passed Stonehenge while hitching. A nice woman got us down to Ilminster then we thought we were stuck but two lifts later and we were in Plymouth. The last lift from an Alf Garnett type – "I was there wasn't I".

The last driver had a broad East London accent and spoke rapidly and loudly. He reminded me of Alf Garnett who was the fictional main character in the contemporary TV sit-com 'Till Death Us Do Part'. Alf was famous for his proud, and often bigoted, East London working-class rants. "I was there wasn't I" was one of his catch phrases.

## HITCHHIKING IN EUROPE IN THE 1970S

In the 1970s hitchhiking was different from today's backpacking. Both require a pack but these days it's typically huge and heavy, and people often carry more than one; not a problem because, almost always, there's reliance on commercial transport for travel between destinations. And when arriving somewhere, today's backpacker is often ushered into a hostel's mini-van and conveyed directly to their accommodation. Conversely, hitchhiking in the 1970s involved long periods of standing on the side of a road, with your thumb stuck out, and hoping to persuade a passing driver to pick you up and transport you gratis along your desired general direction. The unpredictability of this concept meant a couple of distinct differences between the two modes of travel. Hitchhiking often involved long walking distances, so a minimal carrying weight was crucial. Also, there could be days when all options of progressing along your way were exhausted and it would be necessary to find the least objectionable nearby spot to bed down for the night: a train station, a bus shelter, under a tree, or a shopfront doorway. Some self-sufficiency was needed, and it was prudent to carry everything you may need for an impromptu overnight stopover.

More significant differences between the eras affected all forms of travelling. To begin with there was no internet; it would be another twenty years before internet cafes would provide travellers with access to instant communications and information transfer. It took a few more years before mobile phones became truly mobile, and reasonably affordable, but, even then, they were mostly restricted to phone calls and rudimentary email. Smartphones, with their access to data networks, would only become more common another five or so years later still. Not having one of today's ubiquitous smartphones made travelling in the 1970s a different proposition for communications, navigation, and access to general information. It could be difficult sometimes, but often there were advantages: observing and interacting with your surroundings; spontaneity; conversations.

Without a phone in your pocket, you could only make a call from a landline. If you were in a technologically capable country, you may have been able to make a call from a public phone or a telephone exchange (if there were language translated instructions). But making an international landline call could be prohibitively expensive for a budget traveller. To communicate internationally we relied on the significantly slower letters, postcards, and Poste Restante: where a sender could address mail to a person care of a post office. The problem with Poste Restante when hitchhiking was you needed to be sure of your whereabouts a few weeks in advance, which was not always the case.

Google Maps would have been a godsend. The most we could usually carry was a general map of the region and hope to pick up any local maps at tourist information or transport offices. If a country's language didn't use our familiar Roman script any street sign or public direction was just so many hieroglyphics. Instant language translation via a smartphone would have also been very useful, but possibly less fun; and not as satisfying when you had some success.

If credit cards existed, they certainly were not within the orbit of we humble hitchhikers, and no internet meant no ATMs. We relied on traveller's cheques with their associated vagaries: finding somewhere to exchange a cheque at a reasonable rate; judging how far the amount of money you were carrying would keep you funded until the next exchange; but simultaneously not wanting to carry too much cash in case you lost it, or it attracted unwanted attention.

Despite occasional hindrances, hitchhiking in the 1970s was, in most countries, an acceptable way for young internationals to explore Europe. And there were some distinctive benefits. The randomness was adventurous – you didn't know where you could be at the end of any day. You also didn't know who you would meet, except they would almost always be either local to the area you were wandering or, at least, a national of the country you were in. Consequently, you may be alerted to highlights that might not have been discovered along the conventional tourist paths. A corollary of the randomness was the sense of freedom. It can be exhilarating striding down an open road, not knowing where you may be in the next few hours, but completely self-reliant knowing that, if necessary, you have on your back everything you should need.

There were several hitchhiking guidebooks available that provided useful information: where to stay; where to eat; what to see; a few key translations; cultural appreciation. 'Hitch-hiker's guide to Europe' by Ken Walsh was among the most popular that I saw. I tried several times, unsuccessfully, to get my own copy. Eventually my parents posted one to me in Spain.

There were good days and bad days of hitchhiking. You might get to where you intended with little time spent on the side of the road, or you might be stuck in the rain for hours. Also, there were tricks and methods: choose a hitchhiking spot just before a lay-by where a lift could stop safely to pick you up; when attempting to enter a motorway or autostrada it was better to position yourself at the slower traffic area of an on-ramp; and it was better to run to a stopping vehicle, without dawdling. When arriving at the outskirts of a large town or city, jump on the first public bus you come across and it will eventually arrive at a central station. Most often all the services you may need (tourist office, hostel, bank, café) should be nearby. When bus or train transport was cheap, I'd make

use of it – as in Spain. And, when hitchhiking seemed hopeless, a bus or train was a better option – like in parts of France or isolated parts of Cornwall.

Some hitchhikers may have experienced risky or dangerous incidents, but I didn't. And I rarely heard of any problems: certainly nothing gravely serious. It's possible the 1970s was a safer time to hitchhike. Perhaps it was a more trusting era and still influenced by the 'peace & love' mantra of the 1960s. I certainly perceive a sociocultural difference between that era and now, forty plus years later. Social kudos then was attributed more for the length of your hair than the width of your bicep. It seemed a gentler time and, perhaps consequently, safer.

**18 MAR 1975**

*We met a couple of guys in a pub in Plymouth. They said come back to our place in Ivybridge – "ok". We also bought £2 worth of Afghani hash. These guys are on the dole and living in a two-storey £16pw house. They're broke but give us a room for the night, dinner, hash, untold coffees – unreal. We also listen to good music. They took us thru the moors – not much. We left about 2PM and managed to get to Mevagissey and booked into a bed & breakfast. We left the guys a loaf of bread.*

*Mevagissey, South Cornwall*

*View from bar on coast side of bay. Beautiful little fishing village*

*We stayed in B&B up there one street back from wharf*

*These two pictures are looking at each other*

**19 MAR 1975**

*Left Mevagissey about 10AM. A beautiful town, very old (C17th) and built right on the water. We hitched back to St.*

> Austell and got a lift to Truro. Then we were stuck so we got a bus out to the main road. Another lift to Hayle then we walked thru town and got a lift to St Just. St Just reminds me of 'Dr Finlay's Casebook'. Maybe a bit depressing – very grey, but the people are friendly.

The town of St Just was very dark grey and stony. It was reminiscent of the setting of a BBC television drama series of the 1960s ('Dr Finlay's Casebook') which was centred on a general medical practice in a Scottish town of the late 1920s.

**20 MAR 1975**

> We walked 15 miles to St Ives. A really hard walk.

This narrow road followed the stark coastline through bracken-fielded, stone-cottaged farms. It was a cold dark sky and very few cars passed us. Of those few, no drivers were interested in stopping for two males trudging along that lonely route; worse still we sometimes found it difficult to get out of their way because dry-stone walls were built along the road edge. We were hungry, sore, and miserable after the first few miles and then all the way to St Ives.

> St Ives is very nice. A 'younger' place with surf beaches, good surf too. We got a B&B place and decided to have a rest. We went to The Sloop pub and met up with two Pommie hitchhikers and got pissed.

**21 MAR 1975**

> We spent the day walking round St Ives. Everything is closed – out of season. Porthmear beach is really nice with a little beach break. Two very big tides a day. Tonight, we found out we're both broke and the banks are closed tomorrow. John stayed with a girl from the pub and got a boof.

**22 MAR 1975**

> We thought we were stuck for money, but we got some at a building society. We got a bus out to Newquay, and it took all day. Perranporth looked really nice, a lot like Scarborough

> Beach at home. Surfing is pretty big in Newquay. We got a room for £1. Night life is pretty dead.

**23 MAR 1975**

> We started walking out of Newquay. Hitching is hopeless. Then a bus to a little hole called Indian Queens, and started hitching again, but still hopeless. We thought we were there for the night but then we got a lift to London, 300 miles up the M5 in 4 hours, we reached 105mph – the M5 is exciting.

The M5 motorway links the Midlands with South West England. It was my first experience of a multi-carriage motorway. There wasn't anything like it in Western Australia in the 1970s, and certainly no roads there could enable speeds of 105mph with any degree of safety.

**24 MAR 1975**

> We're staying in Queensway.

Queensway is a main street in Bayswater, an area of West London.

> We spent the day in the city getting set for France. I phoned Jeannie, but I got a cold reception. When my 2p ran out I decided to give her a miss and didn't bother to phone back.

To make a call from a phone box in London you needed to insert a twopence coin. After a few minutes, if you wanted to extend the call, you needed to feed in more money, otherwise the call terminated.

Several weeks later I received a letter from Jeannie via my parents in Perth. She wrote that she was "lonely" in London and her tone was a bit maudlin. She went into a rambling explanation of her off-handedness during that phone call: she wasn't keen to reinitiate our relationship because it would only be short-lived when I continued my travels. But, at the time, I assumed she was also young and free-spirited: I thought she was probably anticipating her own new adventures after her skiing holiday in Austria, and perhaps ambivalent about 'us'.

> Colour TV is great – it makes any programme look good.

I hadn't seen Colour TV before; it was introduced across Australia just a few weeks earlier.

## 25 MAR 1975

*We're off to Dover then to France. It took all day to get there via buses & trains. Hitching is hopeless again. This side of London is docks etc., very dirty and poor. Dover YHA was booked out so we decided on a 6:30PM hovercraft to Boulogne.*

*£5.50 Dover to Boulogne
45-minute trip due to rough weather*

The Youth Hostel Association (YHA) was an international group providing lower-priced accommodation primarily for younger patrons. A membership card from the YHA of your home country qualified you to stay at any of the hostels within their wide network; hostel quality varied almost as widely. But youth hostels were reliably and nearly universally available, and a good place to meet similarly-aged travellers from all over the world.

There were a few quirks that might vary from country to country but were generally consistent: you surrendered your membership card at check-in and it was returned to you on check-out; you could only stay a few days and you were obliged to leave the building by mid-morning and couldn't return until late afternoon; there was a curfew which, if infringed, could mean being locked out for the night; and each morning you were required to complete a designated domestic chore after breakfast. What your assigned chore might be was the subject of some uneasy conjecture – the toilets were not favoured. Some hostels, often in the north European countries, were not very different from a two or three-star hotel; sometimes there were no chores required. But I recall a hostel somewhere cold and dark – Cornwall, Wales, or maybe Ireland – where a group of us were inexplicably consigned buckets of potatoes to peel.

*The hovercraft vibrates more than it rocks. A 45-minute trip. We stayed at YHA Boulogne.*

**25/03/1975**
**Postcard from Dover, UK**

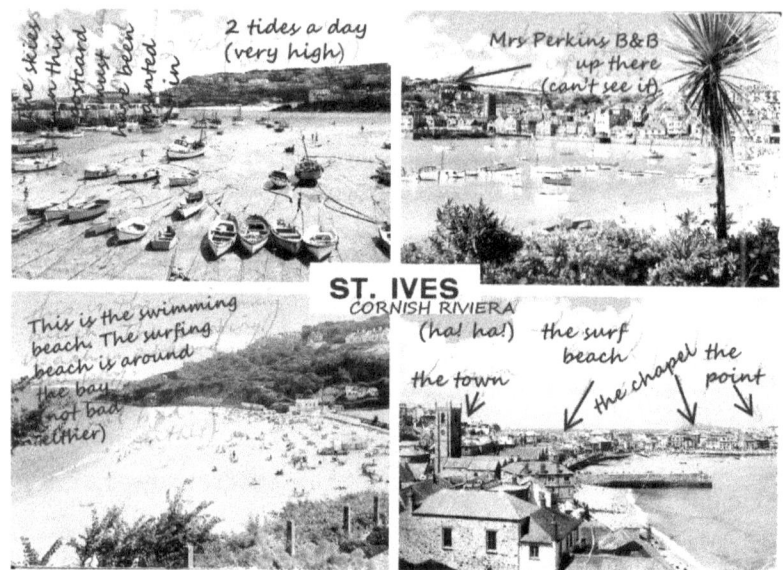

Hi, This is St Ives in Cornwall where we spent about eight days hitching around. Hitching is a great way to travel when it works. At the moment we're on a train to Dover (hitching is too hard here) then we're getting a ferry to Calais. We've had enough of England's weather. I got your letter yesterday and I'll write you one from France. Love Jeff

**26 MAR 1975**

We tried to hitchhike to Paris. It looks like rumours about hitching in France are true. We got a train instead. We arrived in Paris late, and completely lost. Walkabout and the advantage of spoken English would have been handy. We looked up Tony the fashion designer (from the Melbourne barman in January). He couldn't help us so in desperation we checked in for the night into a hotel for a $10 room. Everything is booked for Easter.

**27 MAR 1975**

The language barrier is going to be the biggest obstacle. We

> checked out of the pub and checked out Paris. The Eiffel Tower is huge. Paris is beautiful. Very arty. French patisseries are insane. The Louvre is closed. The Grand Palais is magnificent. I made a big mistake in a bar. I put my cigarette ash in a change tray – not done.

For those unfamiliar with Parisian bars: small saucers placed on the bar are for the barman to deposit a customer's change. The polite and expected behaviour is to leave all or some of your change in the saucer as a gratuity. The barman's already dismissive attitude towards me as a non-Français-speaking vagabond was not improved by my unintentional 'tip' of cigarette ash.

> Paris is very expensive.

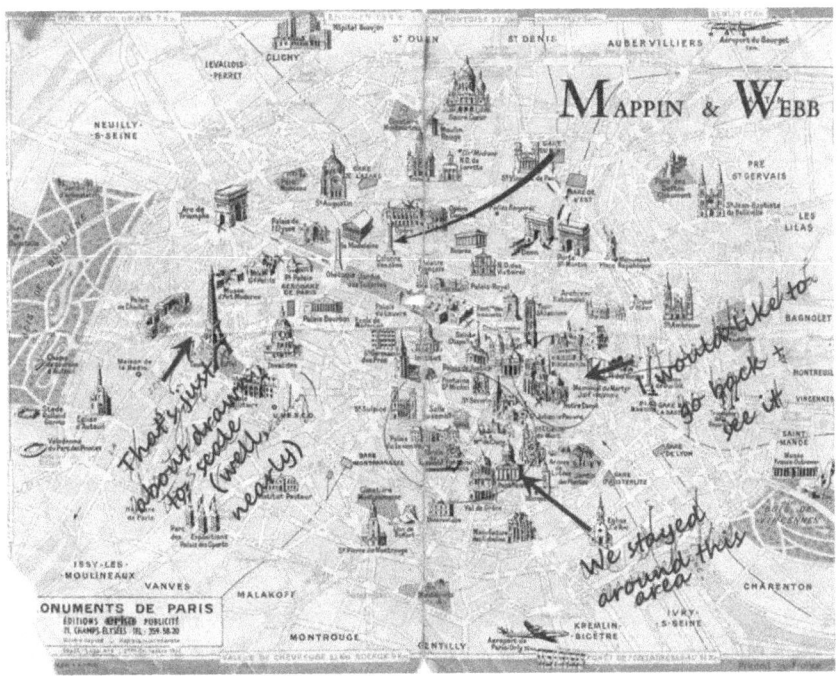

**28 MAR 1975**

> John is travelling on. I'm staying (so I thought).

"so I thought": This diary entry, like a few others, must have been made a few days after the event.

> But all the banks are shut – no money, no accommodation – I grabbed a train south to Lyon and changed a cheque at the

station. I walked into the hostel and who's there — John. I decide to take two days' rest and check out Lyon. It snowed pretty heavy today, my first real snowfall.

**29 MAR 1975**
Lyon is very old — 60BC. A big church on a hill is really nice, so are the Roman theatre ruins. The marketplace is real good and real big. There are acres of market in the morning, and acres of nothing in the afternoon — they just disappear.

**30 MAR 1975**
I tried to hitch out of Lyon, but 3½ hours and no good. I'm getting a bad impression of the French. I grab a train, who's there — John! A nice ride thru the Rhone Valley with mountains all along. I get off at Valence — beautiful. John continues on to Montpellier. I sat in a park waiting for the hostel to open and had a bit of a conversation with a little French tramp ("froid").

It was amazing how much of my high school French returned to me despite it being a subject at which I performed poorly (regretfully it didn't seem relevant at the time). This conversation, like many others, was very simple, included many smiles and hand gestures, and was primarily about the weather. I recalled "froid" was French for "cold".

**Diary Note:**
I've noticed, at least so far in France, that people will chat along happily if they think you're American or English but as soon as you mention you're Aussie they either clam up or become wary. I wonder why?

It was later suggested to me that Australians were unpopular in France then because Australia and New Zealand had instituted International Court proceedings in 1973 against French nuclear weapons tests in the South Pacific; a prosecution which may have been injurious to French national pride.

France

**30/03/1975 (Easter Sunday)**
**Aerogramme from Valence, France**

Bonjour,

at the moment I'm sitting on a sun-drenched park bench in a picturesque little park in the centre of Valence which is a little town in the middle of the Rhône Valley a couple of hundred kilometres from the French Riviera. About 2 miles to the right of me is a towering great cliff with a castle ruin on top of it. This is the start of the Pyrenees Mountains. I'm waiting for the hostel to open because I want to stay here tonight.

The last two nights I stayed at a hostel in Lyon which is the 'gateway to the south of France'. Lyon dates back to Roman times (about 60 BC) and there is an old Roman theatre there. Two nights before Lyon I was in Paris which is a whole lot better than London. I've seen Paris from the top of the Eiffel Tower (which is much bigger than you think), been to the Louvre, Notre Dame, and walked along the Seine.

John and I split up in Paris because I wanted to stay longer. Then we met again in Lyon, split up again, then met again at Lyon station. We came down the Rhône Valley on the same train, but I wanted to see Valence and John has gone on to Avignon.

It's better travelling at your own pace, and you meet a lot of people at the hostels. I'll probably see John again soon anyway because we are both heading for Morocco where it's supposed to be really great and really cheap.

You can get in touch with me through care of Govt of Western Australia, Western Australia House, Strand, London WC2R 0AG. They run a free mail service and will forward any mail to me, so long as I give 12 days' notice. I want to spend a couple of months in south Spain or Morocco, so I'll be getting a room when I find somewhere really nice and settling in for a while. What I would like you to do is send to

WA House., as soon as you can, a copy of Ken Walsh's 'Hitchhikers Guide to Europe' and a couple of packets of Salonpas. I've done something to my left shoulder that hurts like hell – especially when lugging my pack around for too long.

In retrospect it seems a lot of my letters home asked for some type of support from my parents. I suspect it was a way of reassuring myself that I wasn't completely alone in the big wide world. In this request I was asking for some mentholated plasters for applying to my shoulder sprain (Salonpas) and the guidebook I described earlier in **HITCHHIKING IN EUROPE IN THE 1970S**.

Also, although I'm not broke yet, I'm burning up the money a lot faster than I would like (mainly on the train fares because hitchhiking in France is impossible), and if you can somehow get some money to me (maybe postal note) it wouldn't go astray. I've still got $1000 which should see me right for a good couple of months yet but I would feel a lot more secure with a bit more. Anyway, I've decided that when the money goes, I'll go, and I'm not going to live on the smell of an oily rag if it only means a few extra weeks of discomfort. Don't think I'm living like a tourist though. I only have one big meal a day and cook it myself. It's the travelling on trains and buses that kills the budget. I hope the rest of Europe isn't as bad as France for hitchhiking.

Despite a few occasional bouts of acute homesickness, I'm still having a great time and I'll probably be talking for 12 months when I get back trying to tell you what I've seen. I nearly forgot, I got your letter, I'll write to Kim and Dad I'll keep my eye out though nothing much yet.

Au revoir, Jeff

Kim was good long-time friend who had 'done the overland' in 1974. He was a year older than me and the same age as John. I sent him the occasional postcard updating him on my adventure and sometimes I asked for his travel advice.

I was "keeping my eye out" for possible business opportunities at the request of my father. He was an entrepreneurial small businessman who saw my adventure as an opportunity to discover products for the Australian market. In a later letter I try to explain to him the impracticality of that idea.

**31 MAR 1975**

Another hour on the road with nothing, so I got a train to Avignon. Waiting for the next train I decided to check out town and perhaps try hitching. I walked around the castle wall holding the town. On the other side is a beautiful bridge over the Rhone. The town is built inside castles, there's a palace on a cliff. I tried hitching for another hour, then I see a campsite on other side of the river and decide to stay overnight.

**Diary Note:**

Happiness is sitting in the entrance of your tent, snug as a bug in a rug, in Avignon on Rhône, eating pâté and cream cheese on French bread with a litre of milk, a bar of chocolate, and a grapefruit, while listening to my neighbour in the next tent playing a flute. The birds are a chirpin', the sun is a shinin', and it's a beautiful day (stoke!)

**1 APR 1975**

I checked out Avignon yesterday arvo. Beautiful. I met a New Zealand French teacher chick and walked around with her. It was nice to talk to an 'English' person. I tried another hour hitching then got a train to Nimes. I walked thru Nimes and GOT A LIFT! A nice little French student chick ("little English only"). I got to Montpellier and got another lift to Sete. I'll spend the night in my tent in the hostel grounds. The weather is getting better.

**2 APR 1975**

\*\* a day to remember

I spent a total of F8.30. I hitched from Sete to just out of Perpignan with a German couple thru beautiful dry flatlands, then a lift to Perpignan, then a lift to outside Villefranche, climbing higher all the time into the Pyrenees. A young guy and chick bought me a beer, then I got a train to the frontier (for F8.30). A fabulous train ride, tunnels, bridges, snow, and mountains. I met a guy on the train who took me to his home in a huge French villa – a rich family. They gave me dinner, and after they took me to a Spanish disco. A great day!

Their villa was a classic four storeys, elegantly and traditionally furnished, and abutted the cobblestoned main street of a mountain village. The family were formal but very friendly and generously hospitable. They were politely amused when I asked the purpose of their bidet.

**Diary Note:**

It's incredible how you only read back a few days in the diary, yet it seems that it was weeks ago. Just goes to show that travelling is a good way to cram a lot of living into a shorter time.

**3 APR 1975**

The guy's sister drove me over to the Spanish bus stop this morning. Then two buses to Andorra. I met two Swedes who showed me a great pub for 125 pesetas a night. I nearly went crazy in the duty-free shops – LP records for only $3. I met an English couple in the dining room. We went and had a few beers and a music rap. I decide to stay another day and try skiing.

# France - Andorra

**03/04/1975**
**Postcard from France-Spain border**

Hi,

Just a note to let you know that this morning I crossed the frontier into Spain. I'm heading for the tiny country of Andorra. I'm right on top of the Pyrenees Mountains in a valley surrounded by snow-capped peaks. I spent last night with a very rich French family in a huge four-storey villa. I met the son on the train. After Andorra I'm going down the east coast till I find a nice little town to settle down and learn Spanish.

Adios, Jeff

**4 APR 1975**

Miserable weather. A 50 pesetas bus to Soldeu in Andorra and only 250 pesetas for full ski equipment hire, and another 150 pesetas for ski lift rides. Skiing is impossible – dead opposite to surfing. I decide to give it away after many tries.

I was a surfer since I was aged fourteen. With surfing you lean into the direction you want to turn. As a first-time skier I soon discovered, if I leaned into a turn, the skis just slid out from under me. It didn't help that I'd over-estimated my ability and chosen an intermediate skill-level ski run.

I spent the day aiming my skis along short straight sections before throwing myself sideways and backwards while scrambling to clutch onto the ground to prevent myself from tumbling downhill. With great inelegant difficulty I'd then line up the skis and shoot another straight section, and repeat. It took me a torturously long time to get to the bottom of the run while I was being passed by mystified slaloming children. I was also gloveless, and my hands went blue from cold.

> I got sunburnt! Beautiful scenery. Snow is very white.

**04/04/1975**
**Postcards from Andorra**

Hi again,

this is my last night in Andorra (I spent two). Today I went skiing which cost bugger-all as this country is as cheap as chips yet absolutely beautiful. The mountains are so big that this postcard doesn't do them justice?? (a weird sentence, I must be tired). Also, at the moment I'm as homesick as hell. I'll see if I can sleep it off.

Love, Jeff

PS – I can't ski.

## Andorra

My ticket for use of ski lift in Soldeau, Andorra

Skiing is impossible, everything is opposite to surfing.
Still, it was fun at times, had a few laughs

Avignon, France

I just found this card (Avignon) in my bag so I may as well send it off too. I just read over the five postcards I just wrote to you and others and three of them mentioned homesickness — I must shake that attitude. This is the most beautiful French town I saw. It's built inside an old Castle and is very old.

The trees in the circle are part of a magnificent park on a cliff that overlooks the town and the Rhône Valley. All the students hang out there and play guitars and sing songs. I met a New Zealand chick here and we checked out the town together (it was nice to have a conversation in English).

Love Jeff

**5 APR 1975**

I got a coach ride for only about $2 in a luxurious coach with heating and piped music from Andorra to Lleida then across some real Grand Canyon type country following a river through tunnels and overhangs. I got a room in Lleida for 110 pesetas ($1.50) and had dinner at a restaurant for 75 pesetas ($1). Soup, loaf of bread, egg & chips, coffee, and a 13oz bottle wine. It should have been cheap but, after the wine, I was so pissed I gave the waiter a 25 peseta tip.

**6 APR 1975**

I had a hangover!! I've really gone off alcohol – I can't drink anymore. There's no buses today, so I caught a train to Tarragona. A scenic train ride thru 'Sierra type' country. Spain is very mountainous. Tarragona looked nice but there was nowhere to stay. Shat off, so I got a train to Tortosa. I can't find anywhere here either. I was roaming alleys at 11:30PM, looking for somewhere to crash, and the police picked me up and took me to a fonda.

Inexpensive Spanish guesthouses are called 'fondas'.

**7 APR 1975**

I was out of the fonda as quickly as I could – pretty shitty. I looked around town while waiting for the train to Vinarosa. I saw my first semi-trailer bus. The station at Vinarosa is a fair way out of town and I walked in thru a real typical Spanish village. A great little town. Just what I was looking for. Hot weather, a beach, a nice size, bars, disco, town square, cheap food, and accommodation. However, by the end of the afternoon I realised that I'd get bored in a small town like this after two weeks. So, I decided to move on. I also saw the return of the fishing fleet ceremony in the late afternoon.

Although my diary entry describes this as "the return of the fishing fleet" it may have been the more familiar blessing ceremony (before the boats went out to sea) and I'd misinterpreted it. But it was the "late afternoon" which, to my mind, would have been more likely a returning fleet rather than an embarking fleet. Whichever it was, I clearly remember the colourful joyous pageantry with flags, flowers, and music.

**8 APR 1975**

> I decide to move on to Castellon after walking for two hours. I see a camping area sign and follow it. It takes me 5 km out of town. The site is shut. I see a city up ahead and start walking. 8 km later and it's a ghost town — an out-of-season 'Miami'. The only people here are night watchmen and cops. I crashed in a vacant lot surrounded by four-star hotels and magnificent villas. A shitty place — Playa.

I discovered much later that 'playa' is Spanish for 'beach'. I had followed signs to a beach.

**9 APR 1975**

> I woke up feeling pretty dirty. I can't remember when I last had a bath. I found a real town about a mile up the road from 'plastic Playa'. I got a bus to Valencia. I decide that this will do for a mail pickup place. I ask a barman where to find a hotel and he gives me an address of a fonda. It's pretty shitty but it will do till I find something better. I had a beer before dinner and felt a bit pissed — I must be really dried out.

**10 APR 1975**

> I moved to a hotel. It's cheaper, cleaner, and nicer people. Now that I'm settled, I decided to check out the tourist bureau and post office. I bought a copy of The Times, got a seat in a sidewalk café in the sun by the fountain, and caught up on the world news over a Fanta. A nice afternoon. I'm worried about commies in Vietnam and Cambodia.

**10/04/1975**
**Aerogramme from Valencia, Spain**

*Valencia, Spain*

Cathedral the main attraction, not much after Paris

Remains of original town wall. Now a marine museum

Ola!

Well, I finally found a place to settle in for a while – Valencia, Spain. I nearly chose a tiny little village on the coast called Vinaroza. It was just what I was looking for, typically Spanish. Warm, cheap, clean, whitewashed etc, but after one afternoon I realised that after two weeks of it I'd run out of things to do.

Valencia isn't as picturesque but it's just as cheap and has plenty to see and do. I've written to WA House in London and asked them to forward any mail, so if you haven't written to them you can get me here at Post Restante, Valencia, Spain. It's a mail service run by the local post office. I can't remember where I left you with the last instalment of 'Jeff's Continuing Adventures in the Outside World' so I'll tell you about a few things that come to mind. Firstly, Spain isn't my idea of a fascist police state, at least not for tourists.

Spain was still a dictatorship: Francisco Franco ruled Spain from the end of the Spanish Civil War in 1939 until his death in November 1975. Although it was a nationalistic and authoritarian regime there were gradual reforms over the decades of Franco's rule. He restored the monarchy before he died and, later in the 1970s, the King led the Spanish transition to democracy. Although as a foreign backpacker I wasn't directly affected by the politics, I was conscious of the many different security and military uniforms conspicuous within the Spanish crowds, and I was initially a bit shocked by the many visible weapons the authorities were carrying – including machine guns.

The Ministry for Tourism is doing a great job as far as I'm concerned. Transport in luxury airline-type buses costs ridiculously small amounts like 80 pesetas for 120 km rides ($1 is about 70 to 75 pesetas). All the hotels and restaurants are graded by and come under the control of the Ministry. I'm staying at a one-star hotel now for 75 pesetas a night – that's cheaper than youth hostels.

All restaurants must provide a 'menu de dia' (meal of the day) for a set price. They range from 75 to 150 pesetas. The meal must include half a loaf of bread and a third of a litre of wine or half a bottle of beer. Depending on the price you can get two to four courses. The meal I had tonight was eggs done in mayonnaise first, then chicken Maryland, then fruit salad. I drink beer down here because they serve it ice-cold, and I had forgotten how good ice-cold beer could taste. Anyway, it all cost 120 pesetas (about a $1.60). I reckon I should be able to live on about 200 pesetas a day while I'm here.

I got picked up by the cops the other night in Tortosa. I'd got in late and all the hotels and pensiones were either full or closed so I was roaming around about 11PM looking for somewhere to crash and the plainclothes boys picked me up. After I showed them my "passportay" they put me in the back and drove me to a pensione – very nice of them.

I slept in a vacant lot the night before last. What happened was I walked 5 km to a camping ground only to find it was closed. I saw a town in the distance so started walking again. It was dark when I got there, and it was all bloody closed too. It was called Playa and it's the Spanish Miami but in the off-season, they just lock it up. The only people there were night watchmen. So, I spent the night in a vacant lot *surrounded by multi-storey four-star hotels and unbelievably luxurious villas – just me and a couple of million dollars' worth of real estate and buildings.*

*I got a pile of other amusing little anecdotes, but I'll have to write you a letter and tell you about that.*

*Missing you all.*

*Adios, Love Jeff*

**11 APR 1975**

*I checked out the so-called sites – no big deal. The cathedral sickened me - bloody commercial religion. People were cringing over a glass bowl (a sacred chalice), graven images, 'merchants in the house of the Lord'. I'm thinking of heading for Madrid. I'd go crazy staying here for two weeks. I'm very homesick – I had a talk with a gum tree.*

"Gum tree" was my general label for the native and ubiquitous Australian eucalyptus trees. I was surprised to find them in Spain as, up to then, I'd believed they were unique to Australia. Being very homesick at the time, I was a bit emotional when I unexpectedly came across one.

*I've stopped giving tips – 'you gotta be cheeky'. I discovered counter meals – much cheaper. Patata Tortilla is the stuff to eat.*

The small kerbside sawdust-floored Spanish bars were a real find. Early evenings I'd claim a bar stool, order a beer, and feast on the plates of tapas that would be laid out along the bar counter. Patata Tortilla was layers of thinly cut potato inside an omelette and served cold.

**12 APR 1975**

*A Yankee chick at the laundromat talked me into going to a bullfight sometime. I had a nice day at Albufera which is a freshwater lake just out of town. A strip of land between the lake and the sea is a pine forest with some gum trees. It reminded me of Rotto.*

The Spanish climate and geography were reminiscent of south-west

Western Australia. "Rotto" is the common abbreviation of Rottnest, a small holiday island several kilometres off-shore. An area of the island where I used to camp as a child was dotted with pine trees. The heat of the day and the smell of the pines at Albufera brought memories of those camping days flooding back – perhaps another symptom of my increasing homesickness.

*It's concentrated fishing in the river – huge fish. My Spanish is getting pretty good. I bought a loaf of bread in full Spanish. I even got the money right. Had another counter dinner – 40 pesetas. My moustache even grew a bit (I wish!).*

*This is a poor picture of the Albufera, near Valencia, Spain*

*The best part is the river joining the lake and the ocean strip of land in between, which is thick with pine trees. It's a lot like Rottnest*

*The riverbank is thick with fishermen who didn't seem to be catching many fish but, when they did, they were bloody huge*

**13 APR 1975**

*I noticed today how everyone is absorbed in horror comics and pinball. Even the oldies. You also see old guys with very young chicks. I went to the bullfights. I lasted two bulls. I was nearly sick and left early, shaking like a leaf. It was disgusting. The bull isn't given a chance. It's viciously tormented and tortured for ten to fifteen minutes, then brutally slaughtered.*

**Diary Note:**

*Spain – televised bullfights with commentators and action*

replays. The RSPCA would go berserk in Spain.

RSPCA : The Royal Society for the Prevention of Cruelty to Animals.

'Booo, Hisssss'
Not a chance in hell (the bull). He's got about 20 guys and 2 horses to contend with

My ticket to the bull fights in Valencia. They have them every Sunday and 'Festivos'

God knows how many bulls they slaughter each week, but I stayed for about ½ hour and saw two go.
I hated it.

They also have them on TV nearly every night with action replays and commentators. They are very popular with the Spanish

**14 APR 1975**

I got a bus to Requena. I caused a stir – people out here aren't used to foreigners. I found a fonda in a magnificent old 'Castillo'. The front doors were huge pine and brass. My bedroom door was 4' x 6', like out of a castle. At night everybody hangs around the fountain in the central square. Cars stop in the street to talk to the traffic cop. An arc welder working on a job was the centre of attraction.

**Diary Note:**

Walking down a winding Spanish road. Leaning on a stone fence on the side of a hill gazing at the distant mountains while below me a Spanish farmer is harvesting cabbages from his market garden. His wife is hanging out the washing.

**15 APR 1975**

I tried hitchhiking for two hours but no good. I got a train to

*Utiel and tried again. I got put off the road by the cops. So I got an insane bus ride through Ponderosa country, mountains, lakes, tunnels, pines, etc. to a one-horse town Minglanilla. The only bitumen is where the bus comes in. I was a big deal, a pile of little girls showed me the bakery. I got a room in a real brothel for 60 pesetas. The old bastard over-charged me seven pesetas. A woman was plucking a sparrow.*

*'Ponderosa' country. Spain is far from desert country*

*Then again, it ain't all 'Ponderosa'*

'Ponderosa' was a fictional ranch in the 1960s American television series 'Bonanza'. It was set in a pine-treed mountainous landscape, very much like the country I travelled through on my way to Minglanilla – a tiny remote village, smaller than Requena.

It was apparent the locals were even less used to travellers stopping off there, hence my escort of a small tribe of excited little girls. The "brothel" standard of my hotel accommodation also attested to the scant tourist attraction of the village. An enduring memory of the village was a hunched old woman, completely black-clad, perched on a step, and lethargically chatting to neighbours while she absently plucked feathers from a tiny dead sparrow – presumably it was destined for the pot.

**16 APR 1975**

*A big day. A bus trip through to Cuenca. Very hot, dry, and flat for most of the way – a very Australian-like landscape. Also fabulous farm land of rich red loam. Cuenca is built into mountains with two 'Grand Canyon' gorges on either side. Hanging houses eight stories high are built into the cliffs. I* climbed to a Jesus statue on top of a mountain. The view is insane — like an aerial photo. I felt like I could reach down and pick up the buildings. I had a few beers at the bar before dinner, with each beer I got a free small plate of food. I waited until 9PM before dinner and I still caused a stir for eating so early.

**Diary Note:**

I could very easily immigrate to Spain (I think).

*Cuenca, Spain*

This is the tourists' hanging house (Casa Colgados) of Cuenca.
I reckon the best ones are the ones that the people live in.
Some are 8 stories high built into the side of the cliff.
They aren't as level as this one either.

I walked along there (twice)

A side street on the hill in Cuenca. Again, this is for tourists. The real ones are darker, smaller, and dirtier - incredible

**17 APR 1975**

I went berserk today and spent too much money ($6). It started off a pretty shitty day with a train ride through flat uninteresting country to Tarancon where there was bugger all so I tried hitching and got a lift (the first in Spain) to Daganzo 26 kilometres from Madrid, and things are getting expensive already – my room is 125 pesetas. But I had an insane meal for 100 pesetas, including tip. It would have cost $5 in Perth. I drank too much.

*Calle de Alcala was my 'Salida' from the Metro at Puerto del Sol (work that out)*

A five-dollar meal in Perth would have been expensive for me; in 1974 I was grossing about a hundred dollars a week.

**18 APR 1975**

Only 17 pesetas for a bus to Madrid. It was frightening at first to arrive at a big city (popn. 3 ½ million). I got to the train station and I found a map, then a room. Madrid looks like any other city. Campa da Caso has a Disneyland-type amusement park. It looks incredible – I'll go tomorrow night. My room is expensive and one of the shittiest I've had. The Madrid underground is pretty exciting, probably because it's so old and because I don't know the language. I spoke to my first Aussies for a long time.

*Big statue in centre of Madrid*

It would be several years before I was acquainted with Don Quixote de la Mancha and Sancho Panza.

**19 APR 1975**

> It's been raining continually since I got within 10 kms of Madrid. I spent most of the day at the Palacio Real. One of the best palaces in Europe. Fabulous, 2800 rooms – I saw 50. It was used up until the Spanish civil war in 1931.

I must have missed something in the translation here. The Second Republic was proclaimed in 1931; the Civil War was 1936-1939.

> Walls of leather, velvet, silk hand embroidered with silver. Goyas etc, the ceilings are all masterpieces. One table of tiny mosaics took three generations to finish. Chinese porcelain flowers too. Franco put a picture of himself in there – he claimed the families were related!

**20 APR 1975**

> I went to the eighth wonder of the world – Monastery of El Escorial. The Palace was better. I wish I had gone to Valle de los Caídos instead. I saw it from about 15 kilometres away and it still stuck out like dog's balls. There is a snow-capped mountain range out that way too. I went back to Parque de Attractions that night and had a great time. I smashed up on the electric cars being a smart-arse (I thought I was in trouble). I saw a guy walk into a glass wall at the maze – funny. The bob sled ride was insane scary.

*The Palacio Real*
*One of the best in Europe.*
*Magnificent – very extravagant*

Spain

Monastery of Escorial (8th marvel)

The library was the best part (but all the guides spoke Spanish!)

2nd best part was Pantheon of Kings (very spooky)

**21 APR 1975**

I got the train to Toledo – the best town in Spain so far. It's set on a mountain above a river and a thousand years old.

A magnificent cathedral. The back streets are the most narrow, winding, and crooked yet. I stayed in one. At night everyone gathers at the town square where cafes put tables and chairs out. It's things like that missing in Australia. The only bad thing is the tourist shops everywhere. So are the Yanks. I could have bought an unreal sword for $3.

**Postcards sent with my 25/04/1975 Letter from near Alicante, Spain**

*The Cathedral, Toledo*

I bought two postcards of this place because it impressed me so much. It's the Cathedral in Toledo (Spain). The first thing that impressed me was the size. I've drawn a little stick man in to give you a vague idea. Those pillars are about 12 yards apart, and the inside main hall has got 13 of them lengthways and 6 widthways so it's about 168 x 84 yards. That's 

only the main hall, then there are rooms off that all around. The postcard shows the view from standing in the middle looking down half the length.

The other postcard I bought is to show an idea of the detail in the building. That's the second thing that impressed me. Anywhere there's space to carve something, inside and outside, they've done it, in minute detail,

and nothing is repeated. To give you an example, this card is of the choir which is a relatively small area of the Cathedral. The lighter band on top is of stone and every figure is different. The dark band underneath is wood and each panel is a magnificent carved masterpiece depicting a stage in a story.

But this is only a tiny part of it. The altar is even more extravagant. Another thing that impressed me was the Treasury. There's a tower in there about 8 feet tall made of silver, gold, and jewels, all carved in incredibly minute detail of course, and the gold was a gift from Columbus who brought it back from South America. Its monetary value is incalculable. To start with there is an egg-size sapphire on it that is perfectly pure. That alone is priceless. It's not a bad little church. I was impressed.

El Alcazar (fort) in Toledo (Spain).
From what I could gather, this place had something to do with the Civil War. They had reconstructed & fitted it out in original form including a medieval standard infirmary. Very interesting and I must find out more about the war. Who were the goodies? What did the Poms do?

**22 APR 1975**

I bussed to Quintanar and back into the rain. Nothing here. But I was met by some very friendly locals. The chemist spoke English and he got a big kick out of giving me a hand to find the bus station and a pub. The local deli owner gave me a Spanish lesson.

**23 APR 1975**

It rained all day which made it pretty miserable. A longer boring bus ride to Albacete. Nothing here. I had a good time at night though. I'm really getting into the Spanish way of life. That's breakfast nine to eleven, lunch two to four, dinner nine to eleven thirty. Between lunch and dinner (about eight) I go to a café and have one or two beers and a slice of tortilla and watch TV or people playing cards. I watched a great soccer match – Leeds v Barcelona (1–1).

**24 APR 1975**

I bussed all the way to Valencia thru Requena. Nothing of interest. It was great to get a letter from home in Valencia. Like a recharge. I set off for Gandia in very high spirits. I met an English chick on the train and had a chat on the way down. On the bus out to the camping ground the bus conductor asked to see any foreign coins I'd collected over time. I got out a heap from the bottom of my map case. It was pretty funny him getting the bus driver to drive around the block while we sorted thru them. It rained all night but I kept pretty snug in my tent.

**25 APR 1975**

I woke up to the sound of a little old guy yelling at me. I'd pitched my tent in the driveway. I got a lift to Calpe 61 kilometres out from Alicante. The driver gave me an emotional account of the civil war. The Calpe coast is beautiful. A huge rock to the left and cliffs full of houses to the right. Unfortunately, it's very touristy. Not bad surf, though small. I got my laundry done by a Pommie guy. He's been here 24 years – he "can't think in English".

**25/04/1975**
**Letter from near Alicante, Spain**

Hi,

I got your letter and the 'Hitchhikers Guide' yesterday in Valencia. It was great to hear from home, it boosted my spirits. I only stayed in Valencia for four days before I got itchy feet and decided to head inland for two weeks and see Madrid. It was like another trip. Inland Spain is a lot different to coastal Spain. It's a lot gutsier and probably the real Spain, not touristy like the coast. Some of the decrepit little villages I've been stuck in overnight you wouldn't believe, they're incredible. I love Spain and I'm finding it hard to make my way to Morocco. Since I got back to Valencia, I've been heading down the coast again and the country is getting even more beautiful.

My Spanish vocabulary is growing, and I've had a few 'conversations' using English, French, Spanish, pencil &

*paper, hands & feet. While I was in Madrid, I got a copy of The Times to catch up on world news and found out Cambodia has fallen to the communists, and it looks like Saigon will too. So, I was surprised at the tone of your letter. I imagined a state of panic back home with some of the stories I've read here. What's Gough doing about it anyway?*

Gough Whitlam was the Prime Minister of Australia. He was elected in 1972 as the leader of the centre-left Australian Labor Party after twenty-three years of government by the centre-right Liberal Coalition. Whitlam's government was credited with enacting a rapid program of reforms that radically changed Australia's economic, legal, and cultural landscape. Gough, as he was popularly known, thus became a heroic icon to left-leaning people in Australia, including many of the younger generation. His election campaign slogan was pertinent: "It's Time".

When he took office in December 1972, he immediately ceased the balloted military conscription that applied to twenty-year-old males. The previous government had already decided to withdraw troops from the war in Vietnam but Australian involvement in hostilities didn't formally cease until January 1973. I was nineteen years old when conscription ended; John was twenty.

*On more important issues, as you can see, I've discovered Tourist Bureaus and I thought I better send these pamphlets and stuff back before I get smothered in them. My biggest problem at the moment is time. I only seem to get to the next town each day and decide that it looks pretty good and worth checking out. At this rate it'll take 12 months to get to Gibraltar. I get scared I'm going to miss something. I already regret not spending more time in France and I've been thinking about circling back there after Italy.*

*My sore back is better, but my watch has stopped. I'll see if I can get it fixed in Granada. I keep looking for 'something different' for Dad, but it's hard to find anything that would suit Australia. The thing to introduce would be new ideas or culture rather than new things. For instance, in France there was an olive dispenser at one bar that was really good, but I can't imagine an Australian using one. The whole concept of* a bar here is entirely different. It's more of a meeting place than drinking place. Agriculture is very primitive.

When I describe the European agriculture that I'd seen up to then as "primitive", I meant relative to Western Australia where most farming was broad-acre and highly mechanised – as it still is.

The farmer supplies his local village, so he only uses very small farm lots. I've seen some bigger farms on the plains but only from the bus. It's difficult because I'm really not sure what you're looking for. The differences are not in actual goods but in foodstuffs and cultures and customs.

One thing that I reckon would be a big hit in Oz would be French patisseries. These are cake shops that sell very exotic cakes biscuits tarts etc. But, then again, they're using king-size strawberries, cherries etc when strawberries are cheaper than oranges. Still, I'll keep looking, I'll probably have more success in the more industrialised countries, Germany and Holland for instance.

I had a good laugh this morning. I pitched my tent in the dark last night in a camping area where I was the only tent camper there. The rest were campervans. Anyway, I paid that night in case I wanted to leave early in the morning, but the next morning a little old guy woke me up and started ranting and raving at me about something. I couldn't figure it out but I thought he was after more money. So for about 10 minutes I sat in the entrance of my tent peering out at him trying to explain that I paid the night before. When he realised what I was talking about he shook his head and started running around the tent making sounds like a car. I got out of the tent and saw that I had pitched in the driveway. It doesn't sound so funny in print, but it would if you had seen an excited little old guy tearing around your tent going vrum vrum vrum at 6AM!

I'm keeping pretty fit and healthy. I watch my diet and I get plenty of exercise walking and lugging my pack around. Also, because there is rarely any hot water, I usually do a couple of minute's push-ups and stuff in the morning before I have a wash. All in all, I'm still going pretty well. The only bad times are at night after dinner when I can get a bit lonely and homesick.

If it gets too bad I usually go to a bar and buy a beer (10 pesetas) and nurse it through the night in front of the TV. I spent a great night like that the other night watching soccer with all the locals. It's great getting a letter from home so how about sending one to Post Restante Rome. I should be there late May if I pull my finger out and get moving. I won't worry about money until I really need it. It'll come in handy in reserve.

Arrivederci until Roma,

Love Jeff

**26 APR 1975**

I met a Spanish guy on the roadside, and we hitched together — two hours to Alicante. Then alone again and no lifts! I must be the worst hitchhiker in the world. I got the train to Elche to try there. I'm there late and decide to camp. Elche is really lively — rock bands in a park full of palm trees, and a go-kart circuit where they teach kids to drive recklessly. Older kids rip. When out of sight they really thrash them — nearly kill each other. A great young town with kids everywhere

**27 APR 1975**

I hitched out of Elche all the way to Murcia, and I thought things were looking up until I spent the next four hours on the road out of Murcia. I ended up getting a train to Lumbreras which was nothing but a station. A guard put me on the train to Aguilas to spend the night. Aguilas was a bad move! (as I find out tomorrow). Still, it's a pretty coastal town with small surf.

## Spain

**Diary Note:**
> Sometimes the loneliness gets physical – a dull hollow feeling under the ribs.

**28 APR 1975**
> There is no way out of Aguilas! It is at road and rail end. I have to backtrack to Lorca and try again! A bastard of a day. I spent the whole time waiting on the side of the road in the rain, or in a bar, waiting for a bus to a train station. I finally crawled into Baza at ten at night on a super slow train. One bright time was a conversation with a Gary Glitter fan in a bar at Aguilas.

Gary Glitter was a famous 1970s English glam-rock singer. When the enthusiastic young Spanish bar patron discovered I spoke English he assumed I was an English national. He also assumed all English nationals must be avid Gary Glitter fans (Glitter's glam style was an acquired taste and certainly not mine; I preferred the Led Zeppelin style of blues rock).

The Spanish fan's English wasn't great, and my Spanish was very much worse, but I appreciated his company and our spirited 'conversation' – even though it was mostly about the virtues of Gary Glitter.

**29 APR 1975**
> I jumped on a bus first thing. I decided to get to Morocco once and for all. I met a guy on the bus who spoke five languages – an arts student.

He was impressive and entertaining. His English conversation was often involuntarily peppered with words from other languages. When he recognised an error, he would hesitate with a frown, verbalise through a list of possible corrections, then confirm his intended translation before continuing.

> Granada looks great. Very old and a university town. The first signs of a Spanish student movement. The tourist bureau was terrific – they gave me a big pile of stuff including a newspaper. I got a cheap room in a courtyard type building

right on the corner on the first floor. I can roll up the blind and look down the street – great! I went to the movies and saw 'El Coloso en Llamas' ('The Towering Inferno'). I walked home at 1PM in dim deserted side streets with only the sound of my own footsteps (shades of 'Jack the Ripper').

*Granada, Spain*

View from the monastery I stood thereI lived somewhere there

**30 APR 1975**

The Alhambra wasn't much but the Palacio de Generalife was a beautiful layout of gardens buildings and fountains. At night I went to the Spanish cave village of Sacre Monte and saw flamenco dancing.

Cost me 100 psts
Yanks were paying 400 psts

Genuine Spanish Gypsies. One cool guy in the bar wanted to sell me the Alhambra – which looks great at night. Walking home was pretty freaky again.

Spain

*The Alhambra*

*The Alhambra looks great at night*

*The Generalife*

*This place was very beautiful*

*Fountains, goldfish, oranges, roses, statues, the works. Really beautiful.*

**1 MAY 1975**

*I walked right around Granada looking for a way out. I ended up getting a train to Loja where I got a lift with a very spooky French chick to Algeciras. We stopped on the way and had a picnic. Later we slept in her car at Algeciras in a farmer's place. A weird day walking all over the town and her "one with the wind" bit. But it was cheap travel. I thought I was set with a car ride and accommodation through Morocco with a French chick until...*

*A few tourist parties went thru The Alhambra while I was there. The photographers are incredible. They carry ridiculous amounts of equipment & take pictures of everything & anything. Their models are just as funny with their 'natural' poses.*

**2 MAY 1975**

*I caught her going through my pack while I was waiting for her. I left her in Algeciras and went on alone. I met three Argentinians on the ferry — very entertaining guys. I found out Ceuta is still Spain!*

Ceuta was the ferry destination and on the African continent but still a part of Spain; the Spanish-Moroccan border was still a few kilometres to the south-west of the ferry landing.

*I decide to stay and get my pack sorted out and hit the Maroc manana.*

"Maroc manana" was intended to mean "Morocco tomorrow". It was my mangled version of French combined with Spanish.

*It's a big step leaving the ease of Spain. Still, it hit me today that I'm actually going through all of these name places that I write down, so I continue in high spirits.*

## ONE WITH THE WIND IN A CITROEN 2CV

I was hitchhiking out of Loja, Spain, not far from Granada, on my way to Algeciras to catch the ferry to Morocco. A car stopped for me, and I was excited to find the driver of the little Citroen 2CV was an attractive French girl about my age, maybe a few years older. She had a mop of tight-curled blond hair and was wearing lipstick and a short summery dress. Her English was ok (way better than my French) and she told me she was also heading for Morocco to tour for a few weeks' holiday.

We were both a bit excited about our similar travel plans. She was also interested in the logistics of my broader adventure to travel around the world for a year; as well as my means to do so for so long. We puttered along in that odd little car, all exuberance and sunshine. A few times, with a small languid wave to nobody in particular, but to the world in general, she would laugh: "I am one with the sky, I am one with the wind!" It seemed a bit strange to me, but not strange enough to dim the possibilities I was imagining. The promising mood was heightened when we stopped in a layby and, after enjoying a small picnic, we agreed to travel through Morocco together and share expenses.

A few more kilometres down the road we stopped to pick up another hitchhiker. He was Spanish and a bit younger and he piled into the back seat. Those familiar with the Citroen 2CV will know its sparse utilitarian interior, its quirky singular very French character, and its derisory horsepower. The countryside we were travelling through, though not mountainous, was a challenge for the tiny vehicle – especially when loaded with three people and their luggage. Several times the Spaniard and I exchanged anxious glances as the determined, but careless, mademoiselle pushed her little vehicle around steep, sweeping corners; sometimes into over-ambitious over-taking positions. He seemed relieved when we dropped him off close to the outskirts of Algeciras.

After arriving inside the city, we checked at the ferry terminal for the next day's departure times. Then we found a secluded market garden nearby to free-camp overnight in the car. We spent a clumsy and uncomfortable night trying to sleep, and fumble a bit with each other, in the cramped confines of that ridiculous space. The next morning, we wandered around town while waiting for the ferry. It had been a pleasant day. We sat for a while in a café with some fellow travellers; they also seemed unsure of her being "one with the wind". I stayed with them while she went back to the car for something.

She was gone longer than I'd expected so I also went back. I found her deep into my pack with some contents strewn across the front seats. I was stunned, confused, saddened. I didn't ask for an explanation. I gathered up my precious world of belongings and sorted them back into their rightful places in my pack. I recalled her earlier interest in how I could afford to travel for so long; I assumed she was looking for my money. She pleaded innocence and puzzlement, but I strode off to the ferry terminal: determined and alone.

As a walk-on ferry passenger, I queued in a different line to the drive-on passengers. She spied me across the crowded lines and piteously, conspicuously, and perhaps a bit over-dramatically, implored me to join her. I was still too baffled, and somewhat angry, to respond (and probably not sophisticated enough). I stayed mute and stared straight ahead as my queue progressed and distanced us. I was conscious of fellow travellers, especially side-eyeing women, indignant at my unkindness toward the despairing girl.

After boarding the ferry, I didn't see her again. I've reflected since: did I act too impulsively? If I had foreknowledge of my ensuing Moroccan experiences, I might have been more forgiving. Did she have an excuse, however implausible, to search through my things? Did I miss an opportunity to fulfil the dreams I'd dreamt the day before? Could this have been one of those life-choice significant moments and, if I'd decided differently, might I now be living in France and also "one with the wind"?

Or maybe I'd just be destitute in North Africa. We are where we are…

**02/05/1975**
**Aerogramme from Ceuta, Spain**

*Hi!*

*This one is an extra one that I have to get rid of because I'm finally in Morocco (or will be tomorrow) so I have to post this in Spain (a Spanish aerogramme only valid if posted in Spain). I'm not glad to be out of Spain because it is a fabulous country and my favourite so far, it's just that I wondered if I was ever going to get to see the rest of Europe.*

Spain

My last real stay in Spain was Granada where I visited the Gypsy caves of Sacromonte and saw flamenco dancing (real Gypsies). It sounds better than it was, still it was a worthwhile experience. After Granada it only took one lift and one day to get to Algeciras which was just as well because, although the coast from Malaga to Algeciras is really scenic, it is also very built-up and touristy. I got the ferry today from Algeciras to Cueta (I'm technically in Africa) which I thought was in Morocco but found out it is still Spain! The frontier is still 3 km away, so I'm bound to get there tomorrow. Also, while I was in Granada, I wandered through a big department store and noted down the names of a few things that I thought you might be interested in Dad. Names is all I got but maybe the embassy could help you with addresses if any of them are any good. The first and best which I reckon would sell well in Aussie (if they're not already) is an adapter for any TV which turns it into ping-pong, soccer, and four other games. You know what I mean – the games in the pubs. It's called OVERKAL and is a really neat unit. Also, I don't know whether I told you about the coffee machines in Europe before, or the way they make coffee, which is really gutsy coffee, anyway, these machines are in every bar and cafe here. I don't know if they are in Aussie, but one make is LA CIMBALI (it seems to be the most popular).

*General View of Ceuta, Spain (Like it says)*

My description of the leading edge 'ping-pong' and 'soccer' illustrates the embryonic state of computer games in 1975. And my enthusiasm for European café culture was because it was not yet widespread in Australia – at least not in Perth. I also remember being keen about the 'novel' European pastime of alfresco dining. I thought Perth's Mediterranean climate would have been ideal; despite the inescapable bush-flies. However, our local Shire Councils were infamously over-regulating (Western Australia had a reputation for being the 'Nanny State'); it would have been doubtful the Councils of the era would approve the 'unhygienic' idea of serving food on street verges.

Another thing that might sell to flat dwellers is a mini portable washing machine. It's made of plastic, is about 1 cub. ft. in capacity and properly only good for washing socks and undies. It's called JATA by CALOR. It is a pretty cheap looking thing. The sort of thing Majestic Products etc. would sell using those high-pressure TV ads. Sorry I couldn't get any more details but it's not easy trying to convince a department store attendant that you're looking for franchises when you're wearing week-old unwashed clothes, got hair sticking out everywhere, and speaking the wrong language. Let me know if I'm looking for the right things. I'll write again from Marrakesh and let you know what Morocco is like.

Still going fine,
Love Jeff

## 3 MAY 1975

> I met two chicks at the bus depot, Valentine and Julie — a Swiss and a New Zealander. We bussed to the border where the bus left us. We managed a lift to Tetouan. Morocco is very different and exciting. I'm glad of English-speaking company. Every Moroccan is after my money. A bus to Ouezzane took 4½ hours to go 120 km and was very uncomfortable. The countryside is amazingly mountainous. We found a hotel and looked around the markets. Haggling is a gas. I got a leather belt for 60 cents and a block of hash for 50 cents. I tried to get the chicks stoned — but no good.

Valentine was a pretty brunette; slim and tanned; and had a curious habit. While lying on a bed, or legs akimbo on a lounge chair, she would absently wander her hands down the front of her unbuttoned corduroy flairs and idly caress herself. Julie and I would surreptitiously glance askew in mutual Antipodean bewilderment.

**4 MAY 1975**

*Another very big day. We were up at 4:30AM to get a bus thru lush Yallingup-type country to Fez.*

Yallingup is a south-west coastal town in Western Australia. The countryside is semi-lush Mediterranean.

*President Giscard is visiting Fez, so there are big celebrations, including horsemen (they're a rare sight apparently).*

Valéry Giscard d'Estaing was President of France from 1974 to1981.

Years later I learnt I was privileged to have witnessed the centuries old Berber tradition of 'Lab el Baroud' (or 'The Gunpowder Play'): a line of ornately decorated riders charge in unison across a few hundred meters of open ground; then simultaneously fire long muskets from their saddles.

*Saw the horsemen and guns act here, which is a rare sight apparently (also had 100Dm ripped off). The horses are magnificent animals. The medina was the best part*

*Everything is closed because of the visit. We got a room in an expensive hotel (10 dirham) then checked out the carnival. All sorts of gambling games and storytellers (one with live crows and "for Arab ears only"). I met a good guy, Alan – he seems okay – an economics student and going to America. Arabs are*

> very hard to understand — there's always a 10% reserve as they talk.

The "10% reserve" was how I perceived a mutual equivocation when interacting with the Moroccans. This may have been a cultural difference; or it may have been that the people approaching me were angling to rip me off; or it may have just emanated from my fear, justifiably or not, of being ripped off. I was certainly wrong with my blanket attribution to Arabs as I would soon discover in Algeria and Tunisia, and again later in the Middle East.

*Fez, near entrance to Medina. Valentine and me used this as a reference point to get around*

**5 MAY 1975**

> The day started really badly — I was ripped off 100 dirham from the hotel room. Also 'good guy Alan' is a very subtle rip-off merchant. I'm starting to dislike these Moroccans. Many are completely insincere. I reported the theft. We found another hotel near the medina and checked out the shops. They are really crazy about western clothes. Two guys were after my t-shirt. One really ripped shopkeeper (a gas guy) sold me some "good stuff". I got the chicks half ripped (I think). I got really ripped. It wasn't too much fun though — they didn't really get into it.

The hash was quite strong. We puffed away in our shared hotel room and must have bemused the hotel manager when he knocked on the door with some spurious enquiry. Smoke wafted around my blood-shot sheepish façade, into the corridor, as I tried to block the doorway. His appearance didn't help the mood with the girls who were inexperienced with hash and already disappearing into their personal silent paranoias.

## 6 MAY 1975

I said goodbye to Valentine and Julie and took off for Meknes (I missed the bus to Azrou). I really feel alone now. It's worse than other countries because I can't talk to the Arabs (they're all after my money, so there's always an ulterior motive to a conversation). Meknes is the same as all the others. Living is not cheap. It could be if you weren't constantly being ripped off. I'm not having fun, but I guess I'll keep going (I'm having second thoughts though).

## 7 MAY 1975

I got the bus to Rabat. It's really magnificent country. I'd like to do Morocco in a car. I got

*A pretty town and a breathing space between super rip-off places of Fez and Marrakesh*

into a fit of depression. Moroccans are really getting me down with their constant hassling and undisguised contempt. Rabat is a bit less heavy, but still fairly unfriendly though. I saw Hassan's tower. It was a bit comforting to see other tourists – I was beginning to think it was just me and 'them'. I decide to trudge on to Casablanca. I hope things improve.

*Hassan Tower (Rabat)*  *Mohammed V tomb at Hassan Tower*

**8 MAY 1975**

> Casablanca is just a big city. I did a great money deal in the street – I changed 250 dirham for $100 American – nearly $40 profit! I was really happy to get some money back when I jumped in a taxi to Marrakesh – which also looked good. I met a Japanese guy and saw Julie and Valentine again. I bought a good shirt for a good price but got ripped off on a pair of leather sandals that turned out to be made of cardboard. Things are looking up until I checked the changed money. The bastard had switched it! I've got four US dollars! I've lost over forty Australian dollars. It's the last straw, I'm getting the hell out of Morocco as soon as I can. It's my most expensive country so far.

At the time seventy-five Australian cents bought one US dollar. I relived that 'deal' many times afterwards: I was the naïve victim of a classic and likely well-practised switcharoo. It hinged on my gullibility and the similar colours of American one-dollar and twenty-dollar bills. For somebody unfamiliar with the currency it wasn't straightforward to distinguish between the denominations, especially when they were folded several times into a small square.

After the initial approach and deal agreement, my nemesis handed me the five twenty dollar bills we'd negotiated; he asked me to count them. When I'd done so, and satisfied myself all was good, he snatched them away and counted them again right in front of me. Then the clever bit: while still holding the notes he feigned caution that some robbers might be about, and it would be best if the notes were bundled together and hidden somewhere safe – in my boots perhaps; he advised I shouldn't retrieve the money until I was safely a good distance away. He folded the notes and handed me a small wad that I dutifully stuffed into my socks. Then I urgently went looking for a

*Mosque near central Marrakesh*

taxi to Marrakesh where, some hours later, I unfolded my 'windfall' in the safety of my hotel room.

**9 MAY 1975**

> I had to wait until 4PM for a train to Oujda. My desire to get out of Morocco was strengthened by today. Nobody helps. Not even for directions. It's a $12 ticket to get out but it's worth it. A sixteen-hour train trip sitting up. I slept on-and-off. A nice relaxed feeling being separated from the bastards by the window of a moving train. It could be such a nice country too. They think they're smart, but they're stupid.

My diary entry "They think they're smart, but they're stupid" reflects my perplexed anger at the time. Morocco in 1975 was not a prosperous nation and I expect its proximity to Europe, and the fledgling tourist industry, provided rich fodder for less scrupulous Moroccans to exploit their relatively wealthy visitors. It seemed "stupid" to me to abuse those travellers who might provide a basis for profitable business opportunities. But, in time-tempered retrospect, I suppose big-picture future planning would not have been a priority for Moroccans in their day-to-day economic survival when dealing with the tourists. And I was a naïve national of an affluent western nation; I wasn't, at the time, inclined to empathise.

**09/05/1975**
**Letter from Marrakesh, Morocco**

> Hi,
>
> I told you I'd write from Morocco so this is it because I hope to be out of here soon. At the moment I'm waiting for a train to take me 700 km to the border. It's the longest and most expensive single trip I've taken so far but I think it's worth it. I already feel relief knowing that I'll soon be out of Morocco — it's been soul-destroying, depressing and shattering. I was conned, robbed, swindled, cheated, lied to, spat at,

*He's selling water*

sworn at, insulted, and all variations of the above. It'll be a long time before I trust anybody fully again. It's a lousy feeling. I've met three nice people in Morocco in over a week. One New Zealander, one Swiss, and one Japanese (he had been robbed twice in two weeks). Travellers who have been here for any time don't want anything to do with you. I'm going the same way. I feel that the less people I talk to the less I'm going to get ripped off. If it's a lesson that has to be learnt, I think I'd rather not have learnt it. It turns you sour. I've never been so completely on my own.

You can't even ask directions unless you want to pay. Officials like the police, tourist bureaus, station people etc. just won't help you. I just wander around feeling tense and hollow. From kids no more than eight years old to the old people, they all approach you either directly or by starting a sly, insincere conversation and if you refuse either politely or sharply, the kids will swear in English or pick at your pack then run off. The older people usually mutter something in Arabic which is obviously insulting. I just can't find an answer. In other countries I've put bad times down to experience and forgotten them, but here it goes deeper. I've developed a loathing for the whole place and I'm just going to get the hell into Italy as quickly as possible.

Because of Morocco I've lost more than AUD40, nearly two weeks of my holiday, 90% of my faith in people, and 100% of my faith in Moroccans.

My budget was AUD30 a week, so my loss with the money exchange cut into my travel plans. But my letter was an unworldly and unfair rant based on my first experience of a less wealthy nation. Several decades later my wife and I thoroughly enjoyed a two-week self-driving holiday through Morocco – and we met many lovely Moroccan people.

Forgetting Morocco (which I hope I can) I should be in Italy pretty soon because I'm going to go flat out from now on till I get there. I've written to Kim and asked him to let me know if Asia is like Africa and, if it is, then I won't be coming *down through Asia. I'll probably just see more of Europe and fly home from England. But I'd rather go through Asia, and I hope that Asia is okay.*

*I think a fair bit about what I want to do when I get back and I'm pretty sure I'll go to university full-time next year, if I can arrange it. Still, I hope I can see a lot more before home time, I've still got around $750 so I should fit in a few more countries yet. Make sure you get a letter off to me for Post Restante Rome because I could use all of the bucking-up I can get. How about a quick rundown on the world situation? I see all sorts of headlines and it still looks pretty bad in Indochina. Also, home news is great. How's me dawg?*

My "dawg" was my dog, Honey. She was ostensibly mine but, as often happens in families, she was being looked after by my parents.

<u>*Filling up space chit-chat*</u>

*-The train I'm waiting for is the 'express' it takes 16 hours to go 670 km. That's not quite 42 km an hour. Should be some trip.*

*-Did you know that bedbugs are invisible! Every night I'd check the bed for beetles but never saw any. But next morning I itched like hell. I found out here that you can't see the damn things.*

*-Did you know that black market currency conmen in Casablanca are better at the game than I am? I bought USD100 for just over half the exchange rate. The guy handed me a fistful of $20 in Casablanca but when I got to Marrakesh, they'd turned into four one-dollar bills!!*

*Never mind, I'll soon be in Italy,*
*Seeya, Jeff*

**10 MAY 1975**

> I met three guys this morning also leaving Morocco. Apparently south of Marrakesh is the place to go. The Irish guy was as shat off as me. I'm hassled right to the border — I can't get a visa

till after the train goes (an obvious rip-off attempt). And a guy was hassling me for a money change. I finally got a visa and got a bus to the frontier. Algeria is good from the start. The border police are gas. And the bus driver and conductor are really gas. Into Tlemcen and it's beautiful, up in the mountains. Students are everywhere, nice people, and directional signs! I booked into a very expensive hotel with a hot shower. I got super clean and had a delicious soup at a student restaurant with John Lennon on tape. I saw a student debate on TV. Morocco seems miles away.

**11 MAY 1975**

I ballsed around all morning trying to get out of town. Some French guys told me hitching is good. I tried it but they don't seem to like English speaking hitchhikers. I got a bus to Sidi Bel Abbes. I was walking around town when three guys came up and helped me. They took me to a cafe, and I met 'the crew'. One guy said I could stay at his house for three days and he could teach me French. Very friendly guys but that night at his place I found out what they were about – they are homos – there seems to be many in this town.

*Could be anywhere. Arches like this are everywhere*

A contemporary reader, particularly when overlaying current mores and attitudes, might be offended by my label of "homo" and consider it insensitive, or even derogatory. But I contend I was using the term in my diary as a descriptor of men whose sexuality I was aware of but mostly indifferent towards. And I was devoid of any homophobic antipathy.

## Algeria

It wasn't until August 1975 that South Australia became the first State to fully decriminalise homosexual acts; gay culture was still largely obscure in Australia – certainly within my orbit of culturally simple young 'surfies' in isolated Perth. If anybody in our immediate group was questioning their own sexuality, we were unconscious of it – we were struggling enough with our personal pre-occupations, and limited successes, with 'chicks'.

Our only interaction with gay people was when we would sometimes race from the city nightclubs at closing-time to a renowned libertine club we knew that stayed open a bit longer – and we could squeeze in another hour's drinking.

The British TV drama 'The Naked Civil Servant' was released to critical acclaim later in the year; it may provide a contextual defence of my use of the description "homo". The movie was based on an autobiographical book by Quentin Crisp and tells of his life as a flamboyant homosexual living in early twentieth century London. The signature quote from the movie is when Crisp declares himself one of the "stately homos of England".

*The women wear these in Morocco and Algeria. In some towns of Algeria (especially inland towns) they get ridiculous. It's not religious, just custom.*

> I played confused and embarrassed. They took me to a straight friend's place to sleep (phew, a tricky time!). Djalili is a great guy – he digs Elvis Presley and calls chicks "Zorros". His sister is really nice too.

This was a strange episode, not helped by the language barrier. I was welcomed to the first house and met the family. However, shortly after a pleasant dinner, my host began blowing me kisses, winking, and unsubtly indicating it was bedtime. I had seen enough in town earlier to realise what it meant; with a bewildered rebuff, I motioned to leave. This precipitated an uncomfortable reaction from the family – it seemed I had abused their hospitality. The father was summoned, my passport was demanded, and I was curtly interrogated. After a tense half hour, I was taken to a friend's place.

Fortunately, Djalili and his sister, who had lived in Paris, spoke English, and understood our cultural difference. They offered me a bed for the night (of my own) and all was amiably resolved.

Djalili's "Zorros" reference was his joking characterisation of Algerian women's burqas.

I exchanged heaps of addresses today.

Months later, when I arrived back in Perth, I had a letter waiting for me from Djalili.

July 21st 1975
Sidi Bel Abbes
Dear Jeff,
You will never guess what I'm happy, very happy to have a friend like you, but in beginning, forgive me for not writing earlier, I was busy and I've waited for your letter.

I wish, Dear Jeff that you've arrived in good state in your beautiful country. Have you met difficulties in your travel? If you need something tell me, I can send it to you?

Here dear Jeff all the family is in good state and happy, we are in summer, the sun, the seaside, the girls...
Now I must let you, I wish you good luck..
Djalili

**12 MAY 1975**

*I could have stayed because the guys stayed friendly and helpful (though not quite as much) after they realised I wasn't one of them. But I didn't feel comfortable, so I took off for Tiaret. Guys kept trying to con me up on the bus. It gets annoying after a while – now I know what chicks go through.*

One roughly-shaved middle-aged rustic boarded the bus when it was almost empty and chose to share a seat and sat next to me. It may just have been a friendly gesture towards a visitor to his country, but he gradually moved his leg over against mine and continually pawed me to illustrate his conversation. It seemed awkwardly more than just chipper sociability.

*But Algerians are really friendly, a gas little three or four-year-old chick was hanging on to my leg on the bus.*

After my encroaching 'friend' had left the bus, and new passengers had filled more of the seats, a delightful little girl decided I was somebody different and interesting. Without a word she moseyed over, locked me with her big brown eyes, and clasped her arms around my calf. She stayed there for several kilometres with her chin on my knee and a mischievous glint. Her mother, a few seats away, was quietly amused and beamed me a graceful smile.

*No hotel in Tiaret. Walking along a rail line and four winos gave me a drink and chatted. They told me about bathhouses and some kids showed me one. A good, cheap place to stay –*

Oasis just appear out of nowhere. Usually there's a town in them. I was surprised at the amount of water in the Sahara. It probably gets drier further south but, where I was, there was usually an oasis every 100km and at a lot of them there would be surface water. One place had a fair-sized lake. But I wasn't in the centre of the Sahara.

six dinars. Very clean with hot water, mattress, etc. Just need to keep an eye open and my back to the wall.

**13 MAY 1975**

I had a steam bath in the morning. A guy washed my back, it's all very manly and dignified. An experience worth remembering. But I had to spoil it – later I lost my ring down the Tiaret Station shit-house. The ultimate in degradation – up to my neck in shit. An incredibly horrible experience. But I got myself washed and sorted out and got a bus to Ghardaia. Guys at the bathhouse were great. Algerian people are gas.

In a later letter to my parents, I describe my "incredibly horrible experience" in more detail.

**14 MAY 1975**

Last night I got a long bus ride through harsh country that changed every now and then from Grand Canyon to Nullarbor to Sahara.

My Grand Canyon reference was a description of the geography I imagined the iconic USA landmark may look like – deep, dry ravines. Other sections of the landscape we traversed resembled the treeless south central Nullarbor Plain I was familiar with as a Western Australian. And we were on the edge of the Sahara; occasionally we went through sandy desert patches.

I got in late and got a room for three dollars. Algeria is very expensive. Ghardaia is very dry, hot and clean. Rugged beauty. I walked through town. I wandered through a maze of alleyways to a weird tower in the centre. My highlight of the day was climbing

*Where I was wasn't like this everywhere but I passed thru belts of it*

a hill outside of town for a fabulous hour just sitting in the Saharan afternoon looking out over miles of weird country and a beautiful, chequered town below. Moments like that make it all worthwhile.

**Postcard of Ghardaia, Algeria**

This place is just inside the Sahara area of Algeria. I spent a day here. The colours in this picture are all wrong – it's much brighter. I climbed a hill outside of town and got a higher view than this. I sat up there late in the afternoon with a warm, dry wind blowing in my face as I looked way over past the town into the desert which was bright orange. Rugged mountains and canyons all the way to the horizon.

The Sahara is gas. You lose all sense of distance. I thought I'd stroll over to the next hill until I realised it was miles away. Sahara – stinking hot, dry, red, dusty – great.

**15 MAY 1975**

I was up early to get a bus to Biskra. A long bus ride through fabulous country. I saw Nullarbor, sandhills, oasis, Grand Canyon, wild camels, guys getting off the bus miles from nowhere, and great big lakes in the middle of the desert. I got into Biskra and a guy bought me lunch. I tried hitching for a couple of hours (no good), then got a train to Constantine. Crossing the Atlas Mountains was gas. A great wave of mountain. A guy kept feeding me cigarettes on the train. I was really exhausted arriving at Constantine and all the hotels are full. Finally, I met a guy who showed me a dormitory type of hotel, and I swapped yet another address.

This is the Hoggar / Tassili region of Algeria. It's south again of the Sahara. I didn't get down there, but this picture is of country similar to a section of the Atlas Mtns I crossed on the way to Constantine by train. Really cruel country (imagine it in red for the Atlas Mtns). On that train trip we headed into a massive cliff wall shaped like a wave. It must have been hundreds of feet high and stretched from horizon to horizon. I wondered where we were going to go from there, but we went thru a pass and a few tunnels. As we came out of the tunnels there were overhangs above us that must have been hundreds of feet high. Really fabulous. Once thru the pass the train followed a river thru the mountains. Insane.

**16 MAY 1975**

I hassled over the price of the hotel, then I moved to another. I spent a great day in magnificent Constantine. I walked around the outskirts of town following the gorge. The view is absolutely insane. I climbed up to a monument and lay under a pine tree just soaking up the vibes. Everywhere I walked guys say hello or stop and talk or want to help. I swapped a thousand addresses. Met a "calibab"(?) Algerian who showed me the bus station and offered me money!

I still don't know what he meant by referring to himself as a "calibab". The closest I've since guessed is 'Caliban' from Shakespeare's 'The Tempest'; it would fit with the mystical demeanour I thought he was attempting to portray. But it seems more likely it was some Algerian or Arabic reference; or I could have just misheard him.

*The view from the monument is great. Layed under a pine tree here & gazed out over the Atlas Mtns*

Dusk in Constantine – wow! Everybody at the town square, drinking coffee or eating 'crème'. Kids playing soccer and annoying the waiters, old guys with pots of tea sitting around the central statue in the square, students reading and discussing, all while the sun goes down behind the Atlas Mountains – really fabulous!!!

**Diary Note:**

While lying in the wilderness, under a pine tree on the hilltop across the ravine from Constantine, gazing across miles of indescribable Atlas Mountains view, I observe that people are all doing much the same. That is nobody seems to work – they either just stroll around chatting or play dominoes and cards at the local cafe. It occurs to me that in Algeria, and continental Europe, it's the same everywhere (except in the big cities). Their lifestyle is a lot slower than ours. We work our guts out for more 'stuff' and 'relax' by getting pissed after guzzling at the barns we call pubs. These guys just take it easy – drink a bit of coffee, talk with their friends, work a little to keep going but at no neck-breaking rate. Their 'living standard' (possession wise) as we know it is lower, but I think their living standard, in actual quality of life, is better.

'Gorgeous' Constantine.
This is a poor view. The dotted line shows where the real ravine is and the arrow where it turns into a gorge with a sheer drop into the river. I don't think a photo could capture the feeling of leaning over the handrail into that gorge.

**17 MAY 1975**

I hardly slept last night. I'm down with really bad diarrhoea. I tried to get the bus to the frontier but they're full up. I couldn't eat, I could hardly walk. I collapsed back at the hotel, ate a mouthful of tablets and slept all day. I managed to down some greasy chicken for tea. I'd give anything for a fresh meal with no oils, herbs, greases, etc.

**Diary Notes:**

I'm looking for a radio station at night in Constantine when a guy comes on real strong in English! It's bloody Radio Luxembourg! I'm probably getting stations from all over Europe and not knowing it. I just got Germany, and Vatican radio.

I asked about a long line of young guys I saw outside an office in Constantine and was told it would have been a marriage bureau. Apparently finding a wife is difficult. Mostly chicks are veiled after twelve years old (though it's getting better), and there's a complicated marriage ceremony with a bloody sheet thrown to the crowd to prove virginity. If there's no blood, then no marriage. Therefore, chicks hang on to their virginity really tightly. Also, guys have to buy a wife (3 or 400,000 dirham), some rich families as much as one million.

God knows how many times I walked up & down this street looking for a hotel, bathhouse & fruit shop Every 10 feet someone would stop and chat or wish me bon voyage. Algerians are fabulous.

**18 MAY 1975**

Feeling a bit better and I bussed to Annaba. I talked with a guy about Algeria. It's supposedly a socialist country. Into Annaba and I smelt the salt water as soon as we crossed the mountains.

I was very familiar with the smell of the ocean; I'd always lived near to a seacoast.

The Tunisian consulate is closed, and hotels are full. I head for the beach. An old guy in a shop, says, "follow me". His house is next door to an engineers' residence for an English company. A Scottish bloke comes over from the engineers' house and offers me dinner. My first decent meal in ages — lamb chops, chips, salad, peas, wine, tea, brandy, Benson & Hedges, Johnny Cash, Carpenters, draughts, English conversation, bath. A real breather. Feeling a whole lot better, I slept on a

> pile of straw in the old guy's veggie patch. A very hot night and I slept well (I drank too much). At dinner we discussed the possibility of a job with the company. But I'm not really interested.

The "Scottish bloke" was Rob. He lived with his partner Brenda and they both worked nearby for Atkins, a British engineering company contracted to build a refinery for the Algerian government.

They were my introduction to international corporate industry, and I was impressed with their working conditions. Employees were provided with very comfortable accommodation, they received a local living allowance in Algerian dinar, and their GBP salaries were banked in London.

**19 MAY 1975**

> I woke very early and went into town to get a visa for Tunisia. It took most of the morning. No trains or buses to Tunisia until tomorrow. I decide to head back to the old guy's veggie patch to spend the night. I stop on the way and take a rest under a pine tree overlooking the port and a little girl offers me some bread. The old guy welcomes me back. I decide to try the job for the hell of it. I knock on Rob's door and meet all sorts of people, and I start work tomorrow.

**20 MAY 1975**

> I spend a bad night sleeping in a construction site. In the morning I borrow Rob and Brenda's bathroom but still go to work pretty smelly. They offer me two weeks to start at 85 dinar a day and I decide to take it. It's a few weeks of rest with pay, and I can replenish my money and health. I get a bed at an Aussie guy's (Chris) flat. Some trouble with my Algerian visa though. It expires on the 25th. I'll see what happens! The Atkins set up is educational in itself. Renaults are issued like new biros.

I was intrigued by the company's provision of vehicles. Most employees were allocated a new Renault 4 Sedan for their private use. Rob and his colleagues reminisced about weekend Renault-convoy excursions into inland regions; and they planned future trips. On workday mornings I was amused to see lines of Renault 4's, in a variety of pastel colours, puttering towards the refinery.

**21 MAY 1975**

> The job is routine office work from nine to five and I'm wary of it already. It's easy to forget you're in a foreign country (a lot of them do). The dinar is used like Monopoly money. A very Aussie way of living with a lot of boozing. Still, if they offered me a three-month contract, I'd take it for the money. I cooked an omelette for tea and read books, John Paul Sartre looks good, especially 'Nausea'. I notice already there is less adventures to write in the diary.

**22 MAY 1975**

> I can't remember anything significant — just goes to show that office work can be dull. However, this globetrotting employment is definitely the life for me during my twenties. I must get qualified and come back. Some of these guys have really got it wired, like Chris with his several properties.

**23 MAY 1975**

> I tried to get my visa extended but no good. Me, Rob and Brenda had dinner cooked by Chris. A great night with a few beers and talking about travelling. These people have done it all — very inspiring. Also, it was nice, when they talked of Spain and France and Morocco, to throw my two bobs' worth in with a little authority.

By getting "my two bobs' worth in" I meant participating in the dialog. Up to now my default shy character would have deferred to this knowledgeable and relatively sophisticated company, and I would probably have been a bit mute. But, after several months of my own travelling experience, I was beginning to have more self-confidence and I realised I could enjoy contributing to the conversation.

**24 MAY 1975**

I got the train at 7AM to Tunis. Met an English guy Trevor at the border. We played a bit of chess. Algerian dinar can't be changed and are absolutely worthless – "no good". I did a deal and lost half my dinars ($4). Some friends of Trevor met us at the station and showed us a cheap hotel and bought us dinner. We are both broke and must get money in the morning.

**Diary Note:**

A few people now have told me that Morocco gets nice south of Marrakesh where they aren't so used to tourists. Also, the Algerians seem real nice. It looks like my generalisation about Arabs only applies to some Moroccan rip-off merchants.

**25 MAY 1975**

I changed some cheques at The Africa Hotel and went to La Goulette to check out the ferries. The train to La Goulette is very nice and pleasant across the lake. Not much in ferries – only one, and the booking office is closed. Have to wait till tomorrow. A big hailstorm flooded the town. It was a fine day, we went into a cafe and, half an hour later, the town was flooded – real chaos.

Tunis, Tunisia - Main Street. Very touristy place but nice. Best part was little train out to the port and beaches over the lake.

**26 MAY 1975**

There's a third-class ferry trip leaving Tuesday night. We bought tickets — cost $20! We'll get off in Trapani in Sicily. Strolling the town and we met up with the Irish guy (Des) from Oujda in Morocco. Now there are three. We grab the train and head up the coast for a look and to sleep on the beach. We stop off on the way twice, but it's all sterile tourist places. Finally, at the end of the track, we bedded down at La Marsa after a meal and a few beers. It's nice on the beach.

**27 MAY 1975**

Had a swim in the Mediterranean and spent half a day just lying on the beach. Some kids sold us fresh sea urchins and we ate them raw with lemon. We finally got moving and went into Tunis to get Des's ticket then back to La Goulette to wait for the ferry. Hikers are everywhere. Third class on the ferry is surprising. It's very nice with a bar, TV, and three sleeping choices. I almost got nostalgic back on the boat, it reminded me of the S.S Ellinis.

A nice little cruise out of Africa.

# PART II – SUMMER DAYS AS A SWAGGIE[1]

Arriving into Sicily was a relief after North Africa, even though I'd experienced many wonderful moments in Algeria, and some in Tunisia. For the past two months I'd been mostly alone on the road since splitting from John in Paris. I became more skilled at hitchhiking after travelling through France and Spain and, with the weeks of travelling since then, I had become more confident in my ability to make my way generally. Also, particularly after the difficulties I'd experienced in Morocco, Italy immediately seemed easy; travelling through Continental Europe over the following summer months was a joy.

Dependable hitchhiking allowed me to offset the higher European costs of food and travel. I made use of the excellent camping grounds and pitched my tent for inexpensive accommodation. If not pitching my tent, I could stay at one of the many hostels – often at nearly as low cost. And summer in Europe meant there were a lot more kindred travellers to meet, so I was less lonely. There were a few days when I shared travel expenses with a fellow Australian as a passenger in his Kombi and learnt a little of the pros and cons of campervan travel versus hitchhiking.

With my confidence growing my interest in the world broadened; I sought out the historic and artistic riches of Europe; I was vaguely aware of some through my British-Australian education and heritage.

In Amsterdam in late June 1975, I needed a passport photo for a fake student ID card. My nonchalance towards procuring a fake card is indicative of my dwindling innocence; and also, my growing expertise at navigating on my weekly budget of thirty Australian dollars. To me this photo appears to show a bit of travel-earned dishevelment as well as a developing self-reliance and worldliness.

---

[1] Swaggie is an abbreviation of 'Swagman': a 19th century Australian transient labourer who travelled by foot from farm to farm carrying his belongings in a swag (an early bedroll – like a backpack).

**28 MAY 1975**

Woke up and went out on deck to see little islands just off Sicily. We arrived in Trapani which is bloody big and not the little village I was expecting. European civilisation is fabulous. We got a train to Palermo which is really huge and, after all sorts of hassles with a shit-house tourist bureau, we finally got settled in a little camping area in La Favourita. We met a Rhodesian and his Canadian girlfriend. We had tea in the camping area and a few beers and conversation afterwards.

**29 MAY 1975**

We went to climb the mountain near camp, but it was a military installation. We strolled into town and spent a few hours in a cafe listening to good music on the jukebox. The hassle of travelling with others was apparent when we went to get something to eat, and we ended up splitting. Had tea at camp again and a bottle of wine and conversation. I enjoyed the company and ease of hoofing it in Italy (after Africa).

**30 MAY 1975**

They have all got tight schedules and want to get the train straight to Naples. Not me, so we split. It's nice to be alone again and mixing with the local folk. I got a bus out of Palermo and tried hitching. No luck so I got a train to Messina and then a ferry to Italy. The ferry is a huge ship that you're on for half an hour (for 200 lire) with a dining room, bar, etc. I got into San Giovanni still 5 miles from the youth hostel in Scilla when a guy tells me it's shut, so I got a room there.

**31 MAY 1975**

I was up and drank a carton of milk and ate a banana. It was such a nice day I felt like walking to Naples. A beautiful coast road covered in flowers and overlooking fishing boats. I walked a fair way then started hitching. A guy walking stopped and talked and gave me four lemons. Then I got a lift through Tahiti-like country. The driver bought me some cherries then left me on the autostrada — I gave him the lemons. No good on the autostrada so I walked to an off-road and got a small lift to Rosarno and started walking again. I passed a roadside restaurant and some guys called me in and bought me lunch. I hit the road again and strolled through lovely country past olive trees, ferns, and orange groves. I felt like a swaggie, whistling, and singing. I got another lift with a nice guy to the coast. I'd heard so much about Tropea I thought I'd detour and have a look. I got another lift 12 km out of Tropea with a Peruvian guy who invited me to a wedding. I found a camping ground right on the beach and had a swim. I went into town later and had pizza and grappa and listened to music.

Tropea, Italy
View of town from the hill.     Camping area and beach over the back

**1 JUN 1975**

I went up to town and had strawberries and milk for breakfast. Then I went back to the beach and read and swam. I got sunburnt. I had a fish steak lunch. Then I sat under the bar roof in the shade and wrote a letter, drank beer, and chatted with the beach boys. A generally layabout lazy day in the sun — very nice.

*Tropea, Italy (the camping area)*

*The bar & restaurant*     *I climbed the stairs here to town*     *I swam out there to sit in the sun*

*I camped just in there*

**01/06/1975**
**Letter from Tropea, Italy**

Hi!

Here is a description of my last four days in Italy —

I met up with an English guy and an Irish guy in Tunis and we all had tents and pitched them in a pine-treed camping area in Palermo (Sicily). We spent two very nice days drinking cheap beer and talking about travel and anything else that came to mind. We all went separate ways after that, and I got the ferry across to Italy and spent a night in the town over the channel from Sicily.

The next morning was a fantastic day and I felt like walking, so I set out on the wildflower lined coastal road that twisted around the mountains heading in the general direction of Naples. After a while I got a lift through some magnificent country that reminded me of Tahiti. I was dropped off on the autostrada, but I got another short lift straight away to a little country town Rosarno. I walked past a cafe and looked inside but it looked too expensive. I started to walk away when two guys called me in and bought me lunch and beer and a coffee.

I set off walking again feeling like I could walk all the way like this to Rome. I felt completely self-sufficient like a swaggie. It's a fabulous feeling knowing that you're free to walk along until you feel like stopping, carrying your home on your back, and knowing that, if you have to, you can sleep just off the road and eat oranges.

But these Italians won't let you walk too far, and it wasn't long before I got another lift further north and back on the coast. The driver was the second to tell me how good Tropea was, so I thought that was a good enough place to spend the night. He left me about 12 km from Tropea, so I said "ciao", I stuck my thumb out, and a quarter of an hour later I was in Tropea. The guy that gave me the final lift into Tropea was going to his friend's wedding and asked me if I'd like to come along. I wasn't going to miss a chance like that and enthusiastically agreed. He dropped me off at the camping area, but nothing came of the wedding invitation (pity).

Anyway, that's where I am now. This camping area is straight out of a movie. It's no more than 20 yards from the water's edge. In fact, I walk out of my tent into the bar and restaurant area and then onto the beach. It's relatively expensive (800 lire or about a dollar a day – ha ha) It's done out like the South Pacific with grass huts everywhere, cactus, banana trees etc.

I got in yesterday afternoon and decided to spend today here too. This morning I climbed the cliff-side stairs up to the village and had breakfast of milk and strawberries (12 cents a punnet). The village is insane, little winding granite stone roads etc. Last night I had a pizza and then went to the town square and had a glass of grappa (very strong wine/spirit type drink) and listened to the jukebox and watched the gorgeous Italian chicks stroll by. The rest of this morning I spent reading on the beach and now and then jumping into the crystal green Mediterranean. I just walked off the beach into the bar and had a plate of fish steaks and salad and now I'm having a beer and a fag under the grass-roof.

Town from the campground

The bar

The hut area

The type of coastline
Water is over depth about here

  How's all that for fairy-tale living? Believe me I'm having the time of my life. With my jeans rolled up to my knees and the salt drying on my skin, I feel like the main character out of an adventure story.

  That's Italy so far, but so much has happened since I wrote that I haven't yet scratched the surface. If Morocco sounded bad in my last letter it's because it was. I got hassled all the way to the border in Morocco and as soon as I stepped into Algeria it was like taking a deep breath of fresh air. People just changed straight away. I stayed away from the cities in Algeria and headed south into the Sahara. I got as far as Ghardaia — that is just into the fringe of the real Sahara,

## Italy

but I still saw some pretty weird country — that's another place I could write pages about. It'll have to wait and I'll tell you about it one day.

After the Sahara I went north again to Constantine. A magnificently situated city built between, or in the middle of, a gorge that is incredibly deep. Then I went on to Annaba where I came across an English engineering firm (WS Atkins) who have got Poms, Aussies, and New Zealanders all working there. I got four days' work there for 85 dinars a day ($17). I would have stayed but my visa ran out and I couldn't get it extended. I stayed in a flat there with an Aussie guy and had roast dinners and cups of tea and music and countless showers and English conversation. It was a great break after a lot of Arabian Africa. By the way, I couldn't get the money I earned out of the country, so they had it wired to an ANZ Bank in Perth, so I didn't come out of Algeria much richer, but I had a week in an Annaba townhouse and a great time.

After Algeria I just went into Tunis and spent a few days there waiting for the ferry to Italy. I met an English guy there and we just hung around doing nothing in particular. Africa wasn't at all easy, but I've got a lot of memories from it and bad times don't seem to have been so bad when you look back on them.

But I've saved the worst story till last, and I'd rather not tell you about it, but you have to know sooner or later — I lost my opal ring. It's a story I'll remember for a long time and probably goes down as the worst experience of my life, but even that has a funny side when you look back on it over a beer with a few friends (like in Palermo). Anyway, here's how it happened...

In Africa I tied the ring to my racing-bathers cord (it seemed like the safest place) and I spent the night before in Tiaret (Algeria) in a bathhouse (another story) and the next morning I had a bath and wore the ring while my clothes were outside. Then I went down to the train station and went to the toilet. Toilets in Africa are just like a hole in the ground with no traps and are bottomless. While I was there, I thought it would be a good place to tie the ring back onto my bathers. I had my back to the toilet and the hole was about 4 feet away but (you guessed it) I dropped the ring, and it bounced 100 times and went straight down the hole. I just stared at that bloody hole for God knows how long knowing that I had to go in after it.

You can't imagine how much an undisturbed Algerian toilet smells so you have got no idea how much it stinks when you put your arm into one, up past the elbow, and start feeling around. I spent three hellish hours there scraping shit out and sorting through it. I scooped, panned, flushed, and hosed. I was always on the verge of puking, and I got shit in my hair and all over my clothes. The station attendants were pretty helpful, but they wouldn't come near the toilet, it was too filthy for them. I'd reached an all-time low. At one stage I took to it with a pickaxe, but they didn't appreciate that and, seeing that the only way to get to the ring would be to dig up half the station, I had to give it up as lost. They took my name and address, and I went and had a shower, but the smell was with me for the next few days. The very next day I broke out in great nasty welts up both arms that itched like hell and I've still got a few scars from those sores. It broke my bloody heart and if there'd been an airport within 200 miles I'd be home now. But, as I said before, looking back it's all experience and there's nothing I can do about getting back the ring now, but I think it'll be a long time before I forget Tiaret.

What I've been worried about is the insurance. I don't know why but I didn't report it to the police. If Lloyds want verification, the only proof I've got is that the station master has my name and address. It may seem pretty stupid to you *(me not reporting it to the police) but the only excuse I've got is that it's pretty hard to think rationally after something like that. My only thoughts at the time were to get that damn shit out of my hair and get the hell away.*

*Still, that's the past and right now I'm looking forward to taking it easy up to Naples, Rome, Florence, Venice, and Switzerland, back into France, Belgium and Amsterdam. I may even drop back into England and chase a month of work (I've heard reports of good wages in the Midlands). But you can't plan too far ahead (for instance I expected to be in Naples tonight, but I found Tropea). Sorry about that last letter but Morocco is behind me now and, at the moment, I'm having a great time.*

*See you in Rome,*
*Arrivederci, Jeff*

## Losing my opal dress ring in Tiaret, Algeria

I sensed there was something slimy in my hair. But it was better not to stop on the footpath: just keep going. Oncoming people were ushering each other aside, keeping their distance: appalled. I would have been embarrassed if I wasn't so driven – I was desperate to scrub away that disgusting smell…

In my **Letter from Tropea, Italy** I tell my parents that I'd lost my dress ring down a toilet at the train station in Tiaret, Algeria. I left out some details in the letter to avoid causing my parents unnecessary anxiety. Why I persisted in subjecting myself to extreme degradation at that railway station may be better understood if I explain why I put such a high value on the ring.

My parents gave me that opal and gold dress ring for my twenty-first birthday. The set opal was about a square centimetre of translucent gemstone, and it reflected a dazzling array of brilliant blues, greens, and fiery reds and yellows. It was framed with a simple dappled gold band. I would spend idle time toggling the opal stone on my ring finger; fascinated with the kaleidoscope of changing colours – I loved that ring. While I was on my travelling adventure it had special significance as a connection to home, and my family – particularly when I was feeling a bit homesick.

## Italy

In the letter I describe tying the ring to my racing bathers. As I travelled, I sometimes wore a pair of nylon 'speedos' as my underwear. With limited backpack space and weight, it was advantageous having a piece of underwear that I could rinse and dry overnight. The waistband was a nylon tie cord; I would loop my speedos cord through the ring and tuck it down my crotch and out of sight.

The morning after I stayed in the bathhouse a steam bath was an exotic treat; perhaps culturally mandatory. I wore the ring on my finger while I had my bath. Afterwards I intended to get a bus south to Ghardaia, but first I needed to use the nearest public toilet at the train station; it was also an opportunity to reattach the ring to my speedos. People who have travelled away from well-trodden tourist destinations will be familiar with the squat-style toilets I described in my letter. They are commonly found in North Africa, and also in Asia. The Tiaret station toilet was a primitive version: no ceramics, just a hole in a depression formed into a rough concrete floor.

It's difficult to justify those "three hellish hours" – it was a bit 'in for a penny, in for a pound' or, maybe, like a 'boiling frogs' scenario. I suppose I became a bit manic. After I had determined it necessary to ease my hand down that hole and start dredging up shit, and tentatively sift through it, I was committed. As I unsuccessfully "scooped, panned, and flushed" my frenzy increased. After an interminable time, I was kneeling beside a pile of wet putridity with faecal stuff smeared up both arms and above my right elbow; some had splashed onto my clothes. I realised I needed help. The station master must have been perplexed when confronted with a crazed, shit-covered foreigner; I was pointing wildly at my ring-finger and then the toilet while screaming schoolboy-French phrases: "ma mère! mon père!". Using a dubious mix of languages, and some frantic mime, I managed to convey my predicament and desperation. He was sympathetic; he also seemed especially interested when I translated the likely value of the ring into Algerian dinar.

He led me to an external overflow outlet on the outside wall of the toilet, then to a fire hose on the station platform. We formulated a plan where I'd be in the toilet holding the hose down that stinking hole; he would turn on the water and then watch for the ring as the hose water flushed out from the overflow. He was at the tap; I was standing over the hole holding the hose in place. He opened the valve and within seconds the back-pressure exploded; I was covered with a spray of foul sludge. I instantly dropped the hose. I ran to a pickaxe I'd spied earlier.

## Italy

I made for the hole. But the station master, alert to my intentions, insisted I release the axe; I gave up on the ring.

It was my practice, while travelling in others' countries, to show courtesy to the local people by politely giving way to them: I'd wait patiently at the rear in shops; I'd respect orderly queues; I'd step off footpaths to allow oncoming local pedestrians path-wide access. But now, as I furiously and single-mindedly bee-lined to the bathhouse, I forgot any consideration or manners. I stormed, head down and still shit-covered, straight ahead; I was vaguely conscious of the crowd on the footpath parting around me. And, in retrospect, I appreciate they had every good reason to move aside.

My father took my letter from Tropea to my travel insurer in Perth. I had neglected to report the loss to the Algerian police; at the time I was only interested in getting far away quickly. But the insurer paid out the claim based on my letter, which was a win.

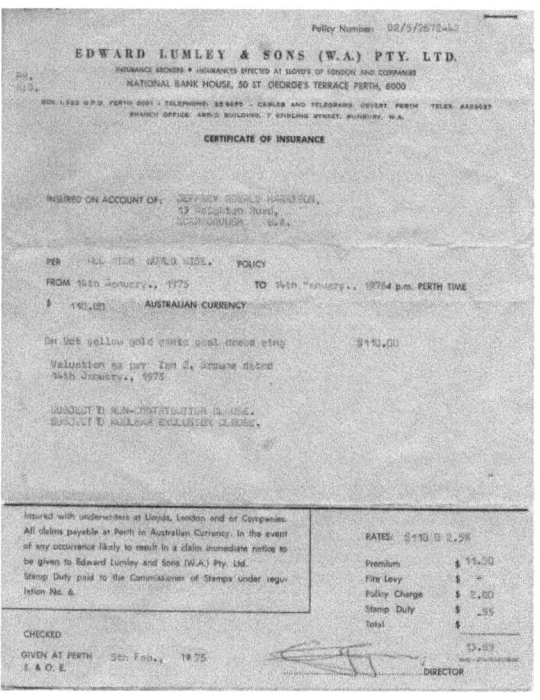

**2 JUN 1975**

> I headed out of Tropea. A series of short lifts to Briatico, then a walk through more Tahiti-like country to Pizzo. I ducked into a roadside bar looking for lunch. I met two American archaeologists. They bought me macaroni, beers, coffee, amaro. I sold my leftover collection of North African coins to an Italian guy. I also got quite drunk. Then the Italian guy gave me a lift to the autostrada. I sobered up walking miles to the next town. Then

*I finally got a few lifts to a beachside town. I bought a pizza and ditched on the beach. A pretty full day.*

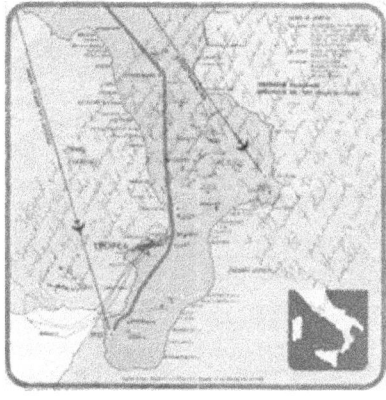

*Stepped into a roadside bar here for something to eat at 11AM. Met 2 American archaeologists who bought me lunch. We were joined by a couple of Italian blokes and had a few beers, played cards and pinball and drank a few coffees and amaros. Left at 4PM pretty drunk. One of the Italian guys bought all my old coins for L3000, gave me a couple of packs of cigarettes, then gave me a lift to the highway. I sat there in the afternoon sun getting drunker and tried to hitchhike.*

*I sang a bit and waved to the cars as they went by. If I didn't like them I'd occasionally give 'em 2 fingers vertical, but mostly I waved.*

**3 JUN 1975**

*I walked off the beach onto the road and continued on my way. Hitching was really shit-house. I walked for miles and miles. I was really tired and depressed when a guy gave me a long lift to Praia a Mare. He explained to me all the benefits of the mafia "they fix mistakes made by the government". He left me on the autostrada. I walked back into Praia a Mare and got a train to Salerno after a few hassles with the train in Sapri. I found a hostel in Salerno. Not bad. I shook hands with a very nice friendly chick in Praia a Mare – phew! Chicks here are gorgeous from young teenagers and up.*

**4 JUN 1975**

*Left the hostel and started walking again. It was built up all the way, so I got a local bus to Pompeii for 190 lire.*

A "built up" area, meaning intense urbanization and traffic, made hitchhiking very difficult, if not impossible.

*The tourist bureau was helpful for a change – I found a campsite and checked out the ruins. Pompeii is a very big town in pretty good shape, though not what I expected. The plaster casts of bodies covered in volcanic ash are pretty spooky. So are parts of the town when you're by yourself (especially underground). A very smart town considering it's only small (by Roman standards) and two thousand years old. A very advanced civilisation. I met some Aussies from Sorrento in the campsite, but they're not over-friendly — they're not desperate for company in their Kombis with wives.*

Sorrento is a suburb not far from my home suburb in Perth. Volkswagen Kombi vans were a common choice among international travellers of Europe in the 1970s; especially favoured by Australians. We hitchhikers, predominately travelling alone, were often keener than the Kombi travellers to socialise with new acquaintances. But this rejection in the campsite in Pompeii was particularly disappointing given I was more than thirteen thousand kilometres from Perth and had met some fellow Western Australians from literally just down the road from my home.

*Looking at the Temple of Jupiter from the Forum*
*The Temple of Apollo is on your left*
*That's Vesuvius behind the Temple of Jupiter*

*The Forum*
*I lined this photo up with the real thing*

## 5 JUN 1975

*I got a train out from Pompeii to Ercalano and then a bus to Mount Vesuvius. The bus ride was to a chairlift, but it was too windy, and it wasn't working. So, I climbed the bastard myself. A very hard climb up ball-bearing slopes. I walked right around the crater. I must have been crazy. But it was great coming down – skiing, the best skiing I've done.*

The slopes of the mountain consisted of gravel stones about the size and shape of 1cm diameter ball-bearings. They made it a slippery climb. Wearing my boots, and by twisting and jumping on the gravel slope, I was able to slide down the mountain slope – like skiing.

*A great view from the top. Naples looks too big to walk through. Back at the campsite the Aussies have gone and now there are some Yanks whose Kombis are incredible. I'm feeling very disillusioned with my pack – it must be nice to have some wheels.*

**Postcard of Vesuvius, Italy**

*The bus to Mount Vesuvius was 600 lire which would have been okay, but it only takes you to a super rip-off joint where*

you have to get a chairlift to the crater for 1400 lire plus a 'compulsory guide'. But the chairlift wasn't working. They weren't getting my 600 lire bus fare for nothing, so I jumped the fence and climbed the damn thing myself. It didn't look too far from the bottom, but it was a bloody hard climb up very loose stones. There wasn't as much activity in the crater as I wanted but it was plenty big enough. There were a couple of hot gas leaks with the best on the far side where no one else went – a bit of rumbling there too. I walked along the ridge that I didn't know was so deep till after I crossed it, also the track disappeared before I got right around so I had to play it by ear for the last bit – all very adventurous. Most fun was coming down the ball-bearing slopes. For about 100m I was really skiing with cutbacks and switches and really flying too. I got a lot of satisfaction by not subsidising the tourist rip-off merchants.

**6 JUN 1975**

I tried hitching at the entrance to the autostrada, but it was no good, so I caught a bus to Naples for a ridiculous 200 lire. From Naples I got an express train to Rome. I couldn't be bothered ballsing around today. I got to a huge hostel in Rome where the main language is English and there are about twenty Aussies and New Zealanders. I had a very big dinner and a beer afterwards and talked with some Malay guys about Asia.

*Rome - a nice photo*

**7 JUN 1975**
*I met a Sydney guy (Ross) and we checked out Rome. The Colosseum is huge. The Forum is a wreck. The Altar of Nations is majestic. The Spanish Steps are a hangout. I saw a fabulous painting of JC there for 100,000 lire.*

I still retain a mental image of this striking portrait of Jesus Christ. It was about 40cm high by 30cm wide with bold brushstrokes of impasto oils: just his face; still wearing a crown of thorns; and with blood dripping down his forehead. But his expression was uncommon; it wasn't the usual placid pious look of forgiveness. Instead, he was very angry; you could say really pissed off. I liked it a lot.

*I had lunch and dinner at the University for only 500 lire. I missed the bus back to my hostel and had to get a taxi – I was in at 11:30PM on the dot.*

Rome was one of the Youth Hostels with strict closing rules. If you missed the closing time you could be locked out, even if you had checked in earlier.

*I also saw St Paul's which is very impressive but why so much wealth! Again, I think something is wrong somewhere with religion.*

**8 JUN 1975**
*Ross went on to Florence with his Eurail Pass.*

A Eurail Pass was a Europe-wide ticket providing first class rail travel. You had to buy it in your home country before you arrived in Europe. They were an easier way to travel around and many Australian and New Zealanders I met had bought one. They were a bit too expensive for me and, being valid for a set period, they didn't suit my open-ended schedule. But they were ideal for those who were travelling for a limited time and needed certainty of transport.

You could sometimes save on accommodation by getting a first-class overnight seat between destinations. A downside was missing out on the random adventure hitchhiking offered: you were less likely to meet the local people; unlikely also to experience the spontaneous joy of having a car stop for you after you'd spent the last several hours slogging along a cold and rain-swept road.

*Vatican City, Italy*

I went back to the Vatican and got blessed by the Pope (even though I could hardly see him). I went on to the Pantheon, which is really something, especially when you realise how old it is. Then to the Trevi Fountain which is pretty smaltzy with 'Three Coins in a Fountain'. The castle and the Sistine Chapel were closed. I went back to the hostel and had a beer and watched some soccer with a South African guy.

**9 JUN 1975**

On a bus to Civitavecchia and a gorgeous little chick gave me her jumper to "take around the world".

I was talking to a very beautiful teenage girl on the bus, and she was fascinated with my adventure; she may have been a little envious. She pulled her beige, fine wool, V-neck jumper over her head and gave it to me and asked that I "take it around the world for her".

It seemed to me like it was her way of vicariously participating in my trip. I cherished that jumper for months afterwards; I was charmed by her gentle dark-eyed melancholy – also her perfume lingered in the fabric.

Then I started a shit-house walk to an autostrada exit (15

km). No bastard will give me a lift. I got to the autostrada and got a lift straight off. He left me on the road and 10 minutes later another lift to Grosseto. I walked through town then another lift with two truckies to the middle of nowhere. They were good blokes; they gave me a map. I was there for half an hour, and ready to bed down, when I waved down an Aussie couple (Tim and Sue). They're looking for cost-sharing riders and so I'll phone them on Thursday to see what we can arrange. I got off at an autostrada exit and got a bus to Pisa – a good travel day (I only spent 50 lire).

**10 JUN 1975**

I stayed in a too expensive pensione, but it was nice. I checked out the Tower and Cathedral in drizzling rain. The Tower leans much more than I thought it would, and the Baptistery was good with a singing guard. I hitched out and only took four lifts to Florence. One lift with stereo Beatles music – gas. I spent late afternoon looking at the town – another Cathedral. This one is made of marble. I ate at the University and met the Yugoslav couple from Rome again.

*The Tower.*
*It leans a hell of a lot more than I expected. The climb to the top is by spiral staircase along the outside wall. Makes for a weird climb with the slant. Behind the Chapel is a huge domed building (Baptistery) where the guard shut the door and did a bit of singing. The echoes were like organ music. Very impressive.*

# Italy

**11 JUN 1975**

A murderous bus ride to town with severe diarrhoea – I nearly shat in the bus seat. I got some miracle pills and went to the Uffizi looking for art. Then to the Museum of History of Science which was really good with Galileo's stuff. I tried to find the modern art gallery but all closed. Florence is nice in the rain. The Ponte Vecchio across the river, flanked by overhanging dull coloured buildings, is a typical Italian view.

**12 JUN 1975**

I booked out of the hostel and headed for the train station. I met lovely Karen again from the night before. I hung around the station with her then phoned Tim and Sue then a train to Sarzana to meet them. They picked me up and took me to their friends' flat (Mario and Wendy). We had a classy fish and chip dinner on the house at their restaurant. I broke an egg – 'life of the party'. In with the ritzy crowd here with their Vogue friends and vacationers.

Yet another impressive Cathedral (tho' I'm getting a bit tired of them). This one's claim to fame is that it's built nearly entirely of marble.

I enjoyed Florence. You could feel the culture oozing out of the brickwork. Spend a few hours in the museums and galleries and feel eligible for a Bachelor of Arts (whatever that is?).

Everybody in the hostel (which is in a museum type building too) sat around dropping names like Lippi, Verrocchio, Botticelli, Leonardo & Michelangelo and discussing cultural things in general.

Nobody knew what they were talking about, but it made you feel pretty good anyway

Florence,
Armillary sphere
Museum of History of Science

Looking down the river at this bridge with over-hanging buildings on both sides, all dull oranges & yellows, with a light drizzle falling & overcast sky. All very Italian. Very romantic city

## BREAKING THE EGG

Mario was Italian and a bit older, in his late thirties or early forties, early balding, and short and stocky. He, with his partner Wendy, owned a flat and restaurant in Sarzana, a coastal town south of Milan. Wendy was a friend and compatriot of my travelling companions, Tim and Sue, and was about the same late twenties age. We were staying overnight, and Mario and Wendy invited us to their restaurant for dinner before we were to leave for Milan the next morning. Several more of their holidaying friends joined us – some also Australian.

As a twenty-one-year-old hitchhiker, on a budget of a hundred deutschmarks a week, I was a bit intimidated by the apparent wealth and sophistication of my fellow dinner guests. Mario, perhaps exercising his alpha status, or famed Italian machismo, added to my discomfort when, periodically, he would hint at my relatively lower social rank; I responded submissively as required.

After the meal, as conversations circulated around the table, Mario grabbed centre-stage and introduced a party trick. He had a raw hen's egg and proposed it was impossible for a person to crush it when compressing directly along its longest axis. The egg was passed around the table to a few people keen to test Mario's conjecture. We were all amazed to see each person fail to break the egg. As the conversation and après dinner wines continued, the egg was placed on the table in front of Mario. But I was still intrigued and, being mostly excluded from the general flow of conversation, I was drawn to the egg. I stood and warily moved across and picked it up.

Mario seemed to prickle at my bravado and the proximity of a lowly blow-in. Undeterred I clasped the egg with it horizontally aligned on the heels of my palms; my fingers interlocked. I pressed but the egg didn't yield. Mario sniggered, somewhat derisively; it spurred me to press harder. The egg rolled in my palms; it became unaligned and lost its structural strength; it smashed between my hands; raw egg sprayed across the table and over Mario's shirt. For an instant he was incensed, but I was rescued by the irreverent Australian sense of humour around the table. Mario read the room and wanly smiled as he wiped away the yolk.

Back at my seat I sat respectfully; silently wishing a hasty end to the remainder of the night, but also appreciating righteous karma, and Mario's newfound disinterest in me.

**13 JUN 1975**

*We left about midday and took Sue up to Milano. It was great screaming down the autostrada, with my arm out the window and my face in the wind, while sitting in comfort and listening to music. There was a nice church in Milano, we didn't see much else. We hung around till about 8PM then left Sue at the station and went on to Como and camped out. So far car riding is expensive. We are looking for another rider though.*

**14 JUN 1975**

*Up early and we checked out the hostel for a rider, but no luck. A beautiful drive around lake country into the Alps. We crossed into Switzerland — it's true about the famous cleanliness. The mountain passes are blocked so we had to put the car on a train for a while. It travelled deep into the Alps to Grindelwald, in the shadow of the Eiger. The youth hostel is a magnificent Swiss villa with a giant chess set. We booked in for the night. A strange hostel — unfriendly, I don't like it,*

# Switzerland

but it's nice.

**15 JUN 1975**

We decided to stay and see the local glacier. A long climb through pine covered Wetterhorn near the Eiger. Indescribable views, a bottomless gorge, we got to the top and watched an avalanche. We threw rocks into the gorge. We found out later there were people down there — didn't kill anyone though. We took off for Berne and found an insane campsite run by the government. A woman gave us a ton of information. We walked around the camp. A very fast river with a guy trout fishing and a squirrel on the grass (a capital city remember). We went into town that night. The tram system is very futuristic. Town is old buildings filled with ultramodern things. Super contrasts.

**JUN 1975**
**Grindelwald, Switzerland**

In the shadow of the incredibly huge Eiger Mountain and flanked by the Wetterhorn and another one. We climbed up *tracks to about 6000 feet (nowhere near the top) and watched avalanches on the glacier. We heard a lot but couldn't see them because they were above the clouds. We saw a few though, underneath. Surprisingly hot up there too. The track got pretty hairy at times — it goes a long way up. Squirrels on the way up in the pine trees. Snow melting in the streams with ice cold water to drink from. We passed a log cabin on the way. They can be rented. It wouldn't have been bad for a few days. It's very nice up there.*

**16 JUN 1975**

*On to Zürich. Went to a museum, we also checked out a department store — insane. We were on the autobahn when a bridge over it had a shopping centre in it. Everything from fresh fruit to stock exchange reports. The "Bells" butcher's shop in Zürich is unreal.*

The retail presentation in Zürich in 1975 was decades more advanced than I'd seen before, including Bells Butchers.

*I bought an open sandwich of mushrooms in mayonnaise and covered in jelly. The department store was incredible — the presentation was out of the 21st century. We stayed at the youth hostel and met two Aussie chicks and we had a chat and a beer. A hotel type hostel. I played some chess, but my game has gone to pot.*

**Diary Note:**

*Question — the museum in Zürich with painting of a horse with a leg cut off?*

*What does it mean?*

I noticed several paintings in the museum depicting a horse with a bloody severed foreleg. I couldn't find an explanation there and I never completely resolved my Diary Note question. There is a legend of the early Middle Ages Emperor Charlemagne founding a church in Zurich after his horse stumbled over an ancient grave.

There is another legend of Saint Eligius: the French patron saint of goldsmiths and blacksmiths. It tells of him amputating his horse's leg before shoeing it. Although that unpleasant saint doesn't have a direct connection to Zurich my recollection of the painting, with the leg more bloody than broken, has me favouring the latter.

**17 JUN 1975**

> We headed up to Rheinfall – Europe's largest waterfall. Millions of tons of water falling 150m with a scary little jetty over the water which was really moving – a giant washing machine! Then we headed off to the Black Forest. Mountains and pine trees with some fabulous views over France. We followed the border along France-Germany. A long drive thru pretty dull country (industrial). We found free camping on a nice peninsula on a lake just off the autobahn. Very peaceful and bloody cold (I saw a firefly – weird!).

**Diary Note:**

> Switzerland is like a model – so incredibly clean and beautiful. I saw a caretaker guy picking up litter at Rheinfall with big tweezers. Switzerland is like looking at a postcard. It's hard to appreciate it is real.

**18 JUN 1975**

> We got up and washed in the ice-cold and headed for Luxembourg. We parked at a busted meter and had a look at the town. We toured the Casemates – deep, dark, musty underground tunnel network of a seventeenth century fortress. Then we watched a slack military parade with soldiers laughing and ballsing around (nice).

A small parade was exercising an uncoordinated routine. It was made up of several very relaxed Luxembourg soldiers with shoulder length hair and beards and moustaches. They were joking and having fun and were the least militaristic military I'd ever seen. I thought they were terrific.

Then on to Mersh and we trudged around a misty rainforest with a brochure and map looking for some prehistoric caves (couldn't find them). Had a beer at a Wimpy Bar and parked off the highway for the night.

**19 JUN 1975**

Woke up in the beautiful Luxembourg Ardennes forest. We headed off to Brussels. No border guards. Same country type as into Luxembourg. We found an English pub and had a few beers. Then to the Grand Palace – very nice. Saw the Manneken Pis – nothing much. After a bit of hassling around the streets we found a camping area out of town. Into the bar and a few more beers before dinner.

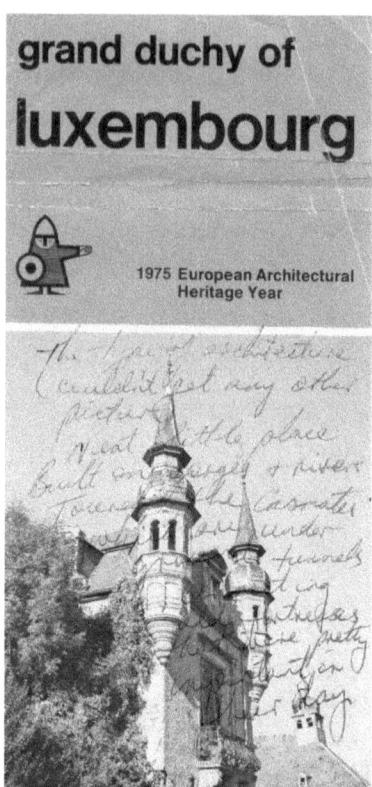

*The type of architecture (couldn't find any other picture). Neat little place built on gorges & rivers. Toured the Casemates which are underground tunnels connecting old fortresses that were important in their day*

**20 JUN 1975**

We checked out the military museum in Brussels. Some of the World War I weapons are nearly medieval. We drove straight into Holland – no border again. Really flat country with canal levels as high as the roads. One point where a canal goes over the road! We booked into a camping area. A zeppelin thing was flying over Amsterdam, and it put on a great light show. We listened to good radio (Neil Young).

## 21 JUN 1975

I went into town with Tim. We wandered around town then checked out the Red Light District in the late afternoon. Then on to VondelPark for a light show – but it was called off. I met a Swedish guy, and we went to the Shaffy Theatre – unreal. Four great acts for 3.5 guilder. Ragtime, a play, Bob Carroll, jazz – a good night.

The Shaffy Theatre (1968-1988) was inside a multi-roomed eighteenth century building and had made a name for itself as a place for avant-garde performances. Bob Carroll was an Irish-American comic performance artist lauded for bringing a social-political dimension to theatre.

## 22 JUN 1975

A couple of hours after I woke up, I scored a deal. It's very strong grass. We had a smoke and spent a few stoned hours in the van listening to Pink Floyd. Then we went to town. I kept having flashes hours later. I booked into a cheaper hotel called H88, and met three guys, Glen, Doug and Norm, and we had a few smokes then went into the Red Light District. Really beautiful chicks, but you have to use a rubber. I crashed at 3AM.

*Amsterdam (beautiful) My favourite city*

*Dam Square. All the freaks hang around here (saw a concert over there on final day.)*

*I stayed in a hostel in a building like these on a canal*

**23 JUN 1975**

I woke late. Then saw the Van Gough Museum — really good. I met a guy off the S.S.Ellinis who didn't want to talk so I left him, went back to the hotel, and had a few drinks. Three Dutch guys took me to a chess club. I played in a simultaneous match. I was beaten by the 1974 Amsterdam champion. All three Dutch guys are better than me, but I won one — rah!

**24 JUN 1975**

Woke late and walked to American Express. I saw Tim again and met his Canadian friends Reg and his wife Dawn — a nice couple. We went back to H88 for dinner and met a friend of Reg's who had a very funny story about his VW van.

*Spent a day here. Really good but I couldn't find 'Starry Night'*

Unfortunately, I didn't record Reg's friend's story at the time, and can't remember it now — just a few more bygone laughs lost in the ether.

I hung around the bar and Glen, Doug and Norm came back so we had a smoke outside. Glen scored out there, so we got very high that night. Met two nice Belgian chicks but I passed out.

**25 JUN 1975**

I spent the day getting a student card from a strung-out guy. A real conman. He forges cards to buy silver to make jewellery *to sell in Spain. While waiting in the queue at the student office he picked a number off the floor to get me served quicker.*

The office used a 'take-a-numbered-ticket' system. My student card salesman searched through discarded tickets on the floor to find a number that advanced me in the queue.

*After dinner I had a blast and went to Shaffy. I didn't get high enough and I couldn't score so I went to bed.*

**26 JUN 1975**

*I visited the Stedelijk modern art Museum — fabulous. 'The Beanery' stole the show.*

'The Beanery' is a walk-in artwork created in 1965 by the American artist Edward Kienholz. I'd not seen anything like it before. It was a small mock-up of a Los Angeles bar that could only accommodate one viewer at a time. You shared the space with dummy customers with clocks for faces. There was a soundtrack of a bar with several noisy conversations and background music. I enjoyed it immensely.

*I also met two Americans, Chris the DJ and Hector the 'Holden Caulfield' mountain climber. They're great guys, Hector is incredible.*

Hector's real name was David, but he called himself Hector. He was a quite highly ranked mountain climber in the USA and was in Europe to climb the Eiger with some Russians. He regaled us with amazing survival stories of his past climbs.

My favourite was when he was in Alaska for an ascent on Mt McKinley and was caught in a snow avalanche. He followed best practice and swam furiously against the oncoming snow to create

*The modern art museum was fantastic (better than Vincent VG)*

a small pocket of space and air around himself. After being tumbled around and disoriented he needed to know which way was up before he could start to dig himself out. He took off his luminescent watch and dropped it. When it flew sideways he knew the opposite side was where he needed to dig to reach the surface. He extricated himself then spent three days trekking back to basecamp; some found remains of a decaying moose carcass for sustenance.

The 'Holden Caulfield' reference was mine because Hector's attitude reminded me of the lead character in J. D. Salinger's novel 'The Catcher in the Rye'.

**27 JUN 1975**

> We went to the Heineken brewery and drank lovely beer. Reg, Chris, Hector and me, we got drunk there, and then onto a bar, then to Stedelijk after a smoke. A very funny day, then back to H88 for more drinking and smoking, then to a club with Margaret and another chick, and Dawn and Chris. A few more beers, then one more, then too many smokes and I blew apart. I nearly collapsed so I went home.

**Postcard from Heineken Brewery in Amsterdam**

I had a ball here. I went with 2 very funny yanks (one disc-jockey & one very dry mountain-climber), also a Canadian. It cost 1 guilder (30c) which is donated to UNICEF. We had an international drinking contest. For 35 minutes you can drink as much as you can. We knocked off 10 beers each, then we hit a bar afterwards. I was drunk all day and had a hell of a lot of laughs.

## 28 JUN 1975

*I wandered around Amsterdam and blew the afternoon, and then met the crew back at H88. We went out to dinner and then on to the Red Light District. Hector was getting out of hand with whiskey – funny as hell. "Blow job in the window", "buy some STUFF!" "is it corned beef?" "red Volkswagen".*

All over Amsterdam, but especially in the famed sex industry area known as the Red Light District, we were constantly and surreptitiously hassled by drug dealers. On this night drunken Hector drew a lot of unwanted attention to them with loud and silly questions.

*We went back to H88, and Chris won 100 guilders on the pokies. So we drank and smoked all night.*

Sometime in the following months I sent Hector a postcard from somewhere. In January, after I was home in Perth, I received a reply from him which described his Eiger climb. His account didn't disappoint me, but I didn't hear from him again.

*Massachusetts, USA*
*1/29/1976*
*Dear Jeff,*
*I'm sorry I've taken so long to write but I've been pretty busy trying to raise money for my next climb. Things went well on the Eiger although the climb was unsuccessful. We got to within 500 feet of the top but had to stop due to severe weather conditions. Even so we didn't go straight down but spent three days in the small ice cave hoping that the storms would break and we could try for the summit.*

*By the third day we were all in bad shape, hungry, tired, and frostbitten. On the way down one of the Russians fell and completely shattered his left leg, the bones of which have been fused together meaning he can never climb again. A few days after getting down the other Russian had six toes amputated from frostbite meaning also that his days of climbing are over. As for myself I escaped without permanent injuries only a few broken ribs. Considering the difficulties, we encountered all of us are grateful to be alive and despite the sufferings they incurred the*

Russians repeatedly write in their letters to me that they feel the expedition was worth all the pain. Both were tremendous mountaineers full of spirit and determination and it is the sport's loss that they will never climb again.

Anyway, I have another expedition planned for September of this year. Myself and a Japanese soloist are joining together for an attempt at Mount Dhaulagiri over in Nepal. Did you get anywhere near it when you were up there? It will be the smallest team ascent ever of any Himalayan peak, so we've got our work cut out for us.

If you are still going to be in Australia around that time maybe I'll leave from California and stop off to see you. I wouldn't mind drinking a few Fosters with you and chasing some of your Aussie girls. Maybe a little surfing too.

Reg and Dawn stopped off at my house for about a week when they got back from Europe. We had a great time in Boston and then they took off for the last leg of their trip back to Vancouver. Chris I've heard from once. He's back at school probably telling stories about the Heineken Brewery and the Red Light District. Your card was well appreciated Jeff and hopefully within a year we'll get together again.

– Hector

**29 JUN 1975**

I got up late and checked out of H88. Said all the goodbyes at American Express. Then I screwed around all afternoon on the wrong side of town and finally got back into the city and got a train a few miles out to Heemskerk and spent a quiet recovering night in a castle hostel with a moat. I had a nice Chinese dinner.

*I stayed in a youth hostel that looked like this (moat too)*

## 30 JUN 1975

The hostel is expensive — three dollars. I walked out onto the road and two lifts later I was on my way to Grou (a yachting village). I got a lift with a guy who took me on a guided tour of the Dykes (30 km of dykes!) Very interesting.

sea water           fresh water
The 30 km dyke in Holland
It's incredible

Grou is a pretty little village on a lake. I camped after fixing the tent. It's nice to be on the road again — the only way to travel.

## 1 JUL 1975

A train back to Leeuwarden and then a long walk through town, then I didn't spend more than 15 minutes on the side of the road nearly all the way into Germany. Then 40 km out of Oldenburg I stopped. One hour on the autobahn, then a 6 km walk on backroads with no lifts. I decided to camp here for the night (Weste something) then I got a lift across the border with some guys in a Mercedes, smoking dope and with a pistol. They were okay guys though.

There were three of them – twenty-somethings; they spoke only a little English. A short distance after crossing the border we pulled over to the side of the road. One of the guys jumped out and briefly scurried about in the bushes.

He returned with a hand pistol and proceeded to wave it around inside the car while speaking to me in either German or Dutch. I just kept smiling. I was more concerned later when we veered off the main road and parked outside a remote house. But we only stopped long enough for one of them to run indoors for a short time; then we continued on our way without incident – much to my relief.

## Germany

**2 JUL 1975**

I got going about 10AM. I sleep long in the tent. I got a short lift to the next town from a nice woman. I had a yoghurt breakfast, then a lift to Bremen. I got plenty of lifts today. I spent my longest time so far on the road up here – nearly an hour! Then a lift to Hamburg which isn't bad, so I decided to stay a day. The hostel is great – up on a hill overlooking the harbour (where I am now).

**02/07/1975 (Shit! Already!!!)**
**Letter from the side of the road, 120 km out of Hamburg, Germany**

Hi!

I forgot when I wrote last, but it must have been Italy which was really good. I saw Pompeii, climbed Vesuvius, threw coins in the Trevi fountain, got blessed by the Pope (ha! ha!), climbed the leaning tower of Pisa, and soaked up culture in Florence. I missed Venice though and I'll have to get it on the way back. I got a lift from an Aussie couple to Pisa, and they were leaving for Amsterdam in a couple of days and wanted a rider to share petrol costs. So, I went on to Florence, then met them in La Spezia. We dropped Sue (the girl) off in Milano to go back to London (she had to have an operation) then we went on through Switzerland, Luxembourg, Belgium to Amsterdam.

We did all that in seven days. Tim (the guy) thought that was great. I thought it was lousy. It's no fun in the van. You become 'van dependent'. I started to get that way after a while, but Tim was a hopeless case. He couldn't stay more than three hours out of the van. While

Saw a couple of these from Belgium & into Holland (they look just like that)

driving past 300-foot waterfalls gushing down the side of a mountain that disappeared into the clouds and I'd say "Jeez, did you see that. That's fantastic, hey?" and he'd say "Yeah that's the first yellow Porsche I've seen in that model" and I'd say "huh?"

Still, Luxembourg and Belgium (especially) didn't have too much to offer anyway, and Switzerland is all scenery and, even flat out down the autostrada, it still takes a long time to pass the Alps. We did stop in Grindelwald though and climbed a mountain trail on the Wetterhorn (near the Eiger). Those mountains are damn big.

In Amsterdam I had a ball. It's the best city I've been in so far. It's like a giant youth centre. I saw jazz concerts, ragtime, plays, a monologue. I even played in a 25 game (simultaneous) chess tournament against the 1974 Amsterdam champion (I was the fourth to lose). I also got into some heavy drinking and stuff with some great people. I'm supposed to meet three of them in Copenhagen in a few days' time — I hope I make it. The three I'm to meet in Copenhagen are Dawn and Reg (Canadian couple) and Chris — an American disc jockey (very funny guy).

The guy that came over with Chris is Hector. He had to go down to Switzerland to meet two Russian guys to climb the Eiger! This Hector is incredible! He's the third top climber in the USA and has got some wild stories. His real name is David *** and they climb around mid-July. It should make the papers so keep an eye out (get me a clipping, please?).

My travel plans have changed again. At the moment they go Germany, Denmark, Sweden, Norway, Scotland, London, then in London I'll sort out the money situation. I've got $500 now so I should have a couple of hundred in London (Scandinavia is bloody expensive). But be prepared to send me the bike money and I might have to go into debt for a couple of hundred as well.

# Germany

I had left my elegant emerald green, but too often nearly lethal, Benelli 250 2C racing motor bike with my parents to sell for me.

For what the fare home from London is I think it's better to go home via Asia. Besides I haven't seen Greece. So, after London the plan is back to Paris (to see the Louvre) then Munich, Austria, Venice, Yugoslavia, Greece (the islands) then island hop across to Turkey up to Istanbul. From there I can get a bus to Delhi for $60. From Delhi it's a couple of hops to Bali then Darwin. It sounds easy on paper! Anyway, that's this week's plan but I'll probably be screaming for money around mid-August no matter where I am. I don't think you'll make Copenhagen but how about a letter in Stockholm.

Say hi to everybody. I've got to get a few letters off soon or I won't have any friends in Perth anymore. It's surprising that even when I've got nothing to do all day but travel, I still can't find time to write. But this is no good. I've been sitting here for half an hour — I must get stuck into it. Hitching, by the way, is the only way to travel. When you get a talkative driver who speaks English you have your own private guided tour for free! And no souvenir selling.

See you up in Scandi 'Stockholm', Jeffsinski

## 3 JUL 1975

I checked out Hamburg — a nice enough city. The best part was the park full of roses and ultramodern stuff. Like water fountains that you can play with (soccer with water-spouts). There's ultramodern department stores of course, but nothing new. A nice night sitting out high on a hill at the front of the hostel overlooking the harbour — it looked like a working model.

There's a sailing lake in the middle of town.
— didn't see any of that

## Germany - Denmark

**Diary Note:**

July (early) a mild summer dusk sitting on a hill out the front of Hamburg youth hostel overlooking the harbour – I'm homesick but I don't want to go home.

**4 JUL 1975**

I started off on a hectic road out of Hamburg.

I thought it might be a bad day then I got a Mercedes ride to the right road for Copenhagen. A few more lifts including one in a Mercedes with a quad tape deck, and another Mercedes ride with a driver's lecture on East German lifestyle, then a really cool Swede gave me a ride from 30 km inside the German border to 12 km out of Copenhagen – a great ride with the Beatles Sgt Peppers playing on cassette tape, and he gave me a chicken and egg lunch. He also bought me a beer on the ferry over. I checked into a sleep-in in Copenhagen – a good day.

Big city but not much like I thought – quite nice really. Reminded me of Perth but not as spacious.
Best part was gardens & park at foot of this tower thing

**5 JUL 1975**

I checked out Copenhagen. A bit of a letdown – their cross between old and new town doesn't work for me. A very moving experience at the Resistance Museum though ("wish me luck as you wave me goodbye...").

This museum emphasised the suffering of the general population of Denmark during the German occupation of World War II. The Vera Lyn wartime song ("Wish Me Luck...") played on continuous loop throughout the small building. The effect of the museum on me was profound. It was, and still is, the most evocative war memorial I've visited. Not least because it avoided the too usual glorification of war and battle histories; instead, it focussed on 'ordinary' people and the prevalent and more mundane tragedies they experienced.

> I walked all over town looking for food. I ended up eating at Tivoli and stayed until twelve to see the fireworks. A beautiful chick sleeping naked next to me at the sleep-in – arrghh!

Compared to now, Denmark in 1975, and Scandinavia generally, was probably even more relatively progressive than most other countries – certainly more than Western Australia. The hostels often had unisex dorms and bathrooms. It was disconcerting for me, as an introverted young man just discovering the wider world, to be confronted with semi-naked young women in the adjoining bunks, or unselfconsciously fully naked in the bathrooms in the mornings.

*Street in Copenhagen*

**6 JUL 1975**

> I moved out, got a bus to the main road, then tore along with ride after ride all the way to Aarhus. I decided to get a train 35 km to Randers (it was getting late) after a guy told me it's a nice place. I arrive and it's too big. I headed for camping and the youth hostel. I follow fucking signs for 5 km in the dark. The camping is in the middle of the forest, way

*Copenhagen was a bit of an anti-climax after Amsterdam. But I suppose it was a nice town. Best part was night at the Tivoli Gardens – a very classy garden and amusement park.*

out of town, and closed. I slept under a pine tree in the car park.

**7 JUL 1975**

I used the camp site facilities (I figure they owe me that much). Again, moving right along. I ended up inland at one time but managed to be in Skagen by 3:30PM. I decided to camp here for a day and rest and clean up before Sweden. It's a big holiday resort where 'two seas meet'. There's not much here really, but I'll stay.

**Diary Note:**

It's a good idea to forget about how to get the next lift or where to stay that night and realise just where you are. Remember, you have been dreaming of these places for years and now you're here. A danger when hitching is to hassle through the country and miss it.

*Cartoon from 'Use It' pamphlet published for travellers in Copenhagen.*
*– Very True*

**8 JUL 1975**

I slept till 11:30AM – great! Then lunch and into town with my washing. I hung out the sleeping bag and pack for air. Everybody is going crazy here because it's about 25°C. All the women are in bikinis. One chick with no bra – nice! I'm the only person with a jumper on.

25°C is a mild day in Perth where summer maximums can often exceed 38°C (the old 100°F).

**9 JUL 1975**

A pleasant and cheap ferry ride from Frederikshavn to Gothenburg (Sweden). Waiting for a tram in the central area I can see the Swedish women really are gorgeous. The men are *all drunk. A very expensive tram fare – $0.40. A small soft drink is $0.40. The hostel $2.50! And I've lost my YHA card.*

*A guy gave me an unclaimed English one at the hostel!*

*I signed it and entered my date of birth; luckily P.G. Phibbs and I didn't look too dissimilar.*

*I also learnt how to play 'Go' from an English street musician.*

**10 JUL 1975**

*I left Gothenburg and got my first lift out to about 30 km, then another lift from a gorgeous Finnish chick in a big Yankee car to 20 km out of Stockholm.*

Among all the different drivers of my many lifts there were some who left a lasting impression. One of them was this distinctive woman who was returning home to Finland.

She was classically beautiful, I'd guess late twenties or early thirties, and her style was extraordinary. She wore a tight-waisted full circle A-line dress and, with her shoulder-length gently curled blonde hair, she could have just stepped off a 1950s rock n' roll dancefloor.

The effect was enhanced by the wide and long-finned American car she was driving. She was almost reclining as she steered one handed, window down, arm out, and her long legs straight out in front. She didn't speak much English so we talked very little – I would have been petrified anyway. It was enough for me to just sit next to her as we careered down the road; me with a big dumb smile on my face.

*I got the underground to town. It's nicer countryside than Denmark. Now that I'm in Stockholm I'm paranoid about going to Kiruna. I just can't make up my mind.*

Kiruna is the northernmost town of Sweden and sits within the Arctic Circle in distant Swedish Lapland. Fellow travellers had recommended it for viewing the Northern Lights (aurora borealis) but it was a very isolated and expensive route.

My dilemma was whether to dedicate the extra time required to get there and, more crucially, a lot of extra expense. Hitchhiking would have been out of the question; not only were the roads and traffic sparse but being on foot in the freezing climate would have been too dangerous. I had to decide if I would forego a rare experience, especially when I was as close as I'd most likely ever be.

> I met an Aussie guy at the station, and we headed out to a camping area.

## 11 JUL 1975

> I ballsed around Stockholm with my pack on my back trying to figure out whether to go to Kiruna or not. I watched chess in the park for most of the day. Then I checked out the Af Chapman – but it was booked out at $3.20 a night!

The Af Chapman was a famous youth hostel. It was a full-rigged three-masted steel ship moored in central Stockholm and fitted out for accommodation.

> Everything is very expensive – over a dollar for a can of meatballs. I bought a tourist travel card for three days' tram fare so I'm here for the next three days – Kiruna looks too bloody hard.

*Youth Hostel over $3 a night (too expensive for me)*
*Nice town, Stockholm*

## Sweden

**12 JUL 1975**

I used my tourist card on the ferry to go and see the Vasa Maritime Museum. It was fairly interesting. Then I spent the afternoon wandering around Grona Lund. I'm a sucker for amusement parks. I saw the yacht of my dreams for sale in the harbour. Later I weaved my way through the drunks back to the campground. I snuck in and pitched my tent for free.

**Diary Note:**

I guess I'll never be satisfied, or at least I'll always have my dreams. I'm finally seeing the world as I've dreamt of doing for years and yet now I dream of owning a yacht and cruising the Pacific Ocean (I suppose it's the same for everybody).

**12/07/1975**
**Aerogramme from Stockholm, Sweden**

Hi!

Well, I made Stockholm a lot sooner than I expected, it only took one day to get from one side of Sweden to the other. Denmark was nice to travel through, though there's not really much there, and Copenhagen was a bit of a letdown after Amsterdam. Stockholm is nice though. It's built on a group of islands and it's a nice mixture of old town and super space-age.

Prices are astronomical too. I'm staying at the camping area, but I can't afford to pitch my tent, so I sleep out (It's fantastic weather – really hot!). The youth hostel cost $3.20 a night, a can of meatballs costs $1.20. Subway fare from the camping area to town is 80 cents each way. I made the mistake of buying fresh fruit the other day, one bunch of grapes and one pear cost a dollar.

Anyway, this is an urgent request letter. Now that I'm here so early I think I'd like to go north into Lapland and see some weird country up there (frozen lakes, glaciers, midnight sun) but it's about 800 miles and I don't feel like hitching that

## Sweden

far in cold, sparse country. So, what I'd like you to try and do, please, is buy me a Eurail Pass for cheap train travel for one month. It shouldn't cost more than $80 (if it does then forget it). The train station would probably be the place to get it.

I'm leaving here on Tuesday 15th, and I should be in Oslo about Friday or Saturday. I don't know how long these letters take to get there and back but could you try and get word to me in Oslo, Norway (Post Restante) about the 20th letting me know how it goes. It would be really great to get up there but if it's too difficult to arrange then don't worry about it. Also, if there's time, could you go to the Youth Hostel Association and see about getting me a replacement membership card (I lost mine in Hamburg). My old card number was W15754. The association is in James Street. No more orders for now, I hope everyone is fine, I'm going well still, see you later,

Love Jeff (the Eskimo)

PS. I won't be sending any more picture parcels back till I'm back in London. Did you see the postage on the last one from Hamburg — 11 marks! That's around four dollars!! The bastard had the stamps on before he told me the price — I nearly blew up Hamburg all over again!

### 13 JUL 1975

Spent the day at the Youth Centre playing chess and ping-pong. I also discussed Australia and Sweden with the manageress. Sweden is still a mystery to me. Apparently "the people get drunk because it's a sin to" and "it's exhibitionism because the people are bored" and "it's too socialistic — 60% tax rate". The youth seem to be returning to the 50s — Pontiacs, Elvis, hanging at the coffee shop.

### 14 JUL 1975

I spent the day in the Cultural Centre. A really good place. A *government-run library with cafeteria, LP records, magazines, newspapers, chess, TV, exhibitions, and beanbags. I listened to John Lennon's 'Walls and Bridges'. I read some books on Australia and a sailing magazine. Also watched some good chess. I still can't decide to stay or go north – my tourist travel card ran out today.*

**15 JUL 1975**

*Spent another day in the Cultural Centre. A chance of student work came up but there's a one month waiting list. I listened to Eric Clapton's new album 'One in Every Crowd' but it's not as good as 'Ocean Boulevard'. I read a nice book – 'Kiss My Firm But Pliant Lips'. Chris and the Austrian are leaving tomorrow too. Ray is staying to sell birds.*

Ray was a singular and interesting compatriot from Queensland; he was also staying at the campground. His laconic manner wasn't easy to decipher, and he impressed me as somebody indifferent to 'the well-trodden path'. He was making a little money selling toy singing birds in the city centre of Stockholm.

Illustrative of 'it's a small world', I met Ray again when I was back in Perth the following year. He had settled there with his partner and had become good friends with Kim: my friend who had 'done the overland' in 1974.

*I'm going to take a few days and stroll over to Oslo.*

**16 JUL 1975**

*I caught a train out of Stockholm to the next town (I used my expired tourist card). My fears of Swedish hitching are confirmed. I walked for miles before a 10 km ride. Then another very long walk into a thunderstorm. I finally got a lift then stepped out of the car and another guy stops and asks me if I'm going his way. He takes me to a hotel-standard hostel in Eskilstuna and then offers to pick me up in the morning. I watched a John Wayne movie at a great hostel.*

Sweden - Norway

**17 JUL 1975**

The guy picked me up and took me to the highway and I got a lift straight off. I forget how it went but I ended up in Karlstad. On the road just out of Orebro I had a nice time picking wild raspberries in a pine forest. I spent the afternoon reading all the newspapers in Karlstad tourist office. I met two Dutch guys (I like the Dutch people) and we went out to a shifty three star camping area.

**18 JUL 1975**

Left the camping area and went to the youth hostel. I cooked a super stew. I met two more Aussie chicks travelling. Played chess with a very good Japanese player. I won one, then fell apart and got slaughtered in the next one. A fairly quiet day.

**19 JUL 1975**

Bought breakfast stuff and after ballsing around with the buses I got out to an exit road. I ate brekkie in the forest, stuck out my thumb and the first car stopped. They're going to Oslo but I got off in Arjang to hire a canoe and go into the lakes for a few days. All canoes were booked out so back on the road all afternoon. Finally two lifts and into Oslo. First person I meet is a drunken morbid guy. Then I meet a German guitar player guy and spent the night in the hostel listing to good folk music jams.

**20 JUL 1975**

Everything is closed in Oslo. Finally got eats in the afternoon then on to

Beautiful park. Best part of Oslo. Sat down there & fixed my thongs

*Frognerparken with great people statues.*

Frogner Park is a forty-five-hectare public park in west Oslo. It's home to a permanent sculpture installation created between 1924 and 1943 by a single artist: Gustav Vigeland.

It's Norway's most popular tourist attraction. The statues are predominately of naked people in surprising and amusing poses. I thought it was fabulous and I spent several enjoyable hours there.

*A telegram for me at the Post Office – no Eurail Pass so no north cape. I got caught in a tram door – funny. Back at the hostel I kidded around with the hostel reception chick about "dull Oslo" with everything closed, so she gave me a parcel of Norwegian kindergarten games to brighten my day.*

**21 JUL 1975**

*Checked out the museums – Kon Tiki, Arctic expedition, Viking ships. The Vikings really knew how to build boats. Then back to town and saw the town hall and another park. Back to the hostel and I met an Israeli guy who said he was "spying on Arabs". Pretty funny, but I didn't laugh.*

**22 JUL 1975**

*I got a bus out of Oslo then a lift to Drammen, then another one to just out of Larvik, then my luck ran out. Two hours in the rain before I caught a bus to anywhere, then a train and another bus to a hostel at Kragero. I met a German guy who speaks American. We had a good rap about everything. Nice little town this – it reminds me of Mevagissey in England.*

**23 JUL 1975**

*I walked into town (I saw guys pulling in some big fish from a little boat) and got a bus out to the highway. I walked a few miles then got a long lift to Arendal, then a short one to 30 km from Kristiansand. All this in the rain. I finally got a bus to Kristiansand and a hostel. I'm tired of the rain and bad* hitching in Norway – high transport prices don't help. Also, just plain tired.

**Diary Note:**
Australian sultanas, pears, apricots and New Zealand apples are all through Norway.

**24 JUL 1975**
The day started with a bang. I got picked up by the press and interviewed while getting a lift. Pictures too, but they only drove me a few kilometres to the edge of town! Two more short lifts then nothing but rain and passing comedians. I was only 50 km from where I started six hours ago so I got a bus to Flekkefjord. It went through some really nice country – mountains and pine trees and lakes. Flekkefjord is a tiny little wooden village in a narrow valley fjord. Narrow streets, steep roofs, putt-putt boats, fisherfolk. The Grand Hotel is fantastic. It's made of wood with two towers. There was a nice cat at the hostel.

**25 JUL 1975**
Got the paper and I made the front page with a photo and a big story. Really stoked. I showed all the drivers. I even got fairly easily to Stavanger (maybe they read the paper). Fantastic country through here, very rugged. Stavanger is a nice town especially the waterfront. But there's no ferry to England soon, and anyway

*The market and old church*
*Old port part of town is very Norwegian – all wood & fishing*

it's over $50. I'll go on to Sand. I had my article translated at  the camping ground and the tourist bureau. A bit of bullshit but a nice write-up anyway.

"Jeg Elsker A Haike" – I Love to Hike. The story was more about the writer's idealised portrait of an Australian hitchhiker (or what he thought was his readers') and less about what I'd actually related to him. I'm described as relishing the "outdoor life" and shunning "dusty museums". My real interest in, and enjoyment of, museums and galleries belied that idea, and I didn't suggest it!

**26 JUL 1975**

Spent the morning in the harbour waiting for the Sand ferry. Then four hours through fjords. Not spectacular but beautiful. I met a guy (Eivind) who offered to drive me to the next ferry, then to the youth hostel. The ferry was closed so he suggests I walk to the next town with him over the mountains (two days' hike). "Ok", and we set off into Norwegian wilderness. This guy is a real nature freak – "man is a fat pig". It's incredible country. I was expecting Julie Andrews to come bounding over the next hill.

My reference to the famous opening scene of the movie 'The Sound of Music'.

10:30PM and it's just getting dark. We arrive at a mountain cottage run for hikers by three very nice young girls. The cottage is on a lake in a valley of mountains with patches of snow. We have a meal of home-made bread, butter, and jam. The sun setting on one horizon behind the mountains and the full moon coming up on the other and reflecting in the lake!!

**27 JUL 1975**

I slept like a baby. Up and wash in the ice-water lake. Then a huge home-made breakfast and we set off at 9AM. The first two hours were incredible. Scenery is insane and an exhilarating

*We didn't go around these mountains but over them.*
*This is the hike country (take out all signs of civilization)*

> feeling of back-to-nature and self-dependence. We crossed streams, snow drifts, and climbed mountains. I fell into a hole on one snowdrift — close to an ice-cold swim. Also bridges of planks and cable. Then we started meeting people coming the other way which took some glamour out of it, but still fantastic. We rested for lunch and a sock change before the mountain assault. We left the 'path' and headed up, dumped our packs, then climbed 1600 metres to the summit. Bad luck as clouds came in and tried to kill the view but it was still incredible standing 'on top of the world' in a cloudy mist — weird.

My diary entry of "weird" inadequately describes this experience; it was more personally profound. A few days later I recorded a deeper explanation of its impact in my notepad.

> Then down to a mostel for fruit soup and rest for the night, we got in about 4:30PM. The mostel is run on a trust basis — no warden.

A mostel is a small mountain shack providing sparse overnight shelter for hikers. They are lightly stocked with a few non-perishable food items that hikers can purchase using an honour system.

'Fruktsuppe' was new to me. It was a sachet of dried and mostly powdered fruit that created a sweet thin soup when mixed with hot water. I suppose the fructose was beneficial as a quick carbohydrate replacement.

**28 JUL 1975**

> We had breakfast and took off at 9AM. It's tamer country now but still beautiful and far from tame by Aussie standards.

I meant here to differentiate between the less mountainous landscape we were then walking through and the flat Western Australian landscape I was familiar with.

> I parted company with Eivind and arrived at a lake (Suldalsvatnet) about 11:30AM and waited for the 4PM ferry. I just lazed around the jetty, wrote, read, ate, slept, sunbaked,

bathed my feet, washed socks – a nice afternoon. Then ferried to Nesflaten.

There's no bank and I have no money, so I can't afford the hostel. I had a little bit of food, and it's 20 km to the next town, so I started walking. After 5 km and no cars I finally got a lift from the first car to Roldal, and I found a camping area.

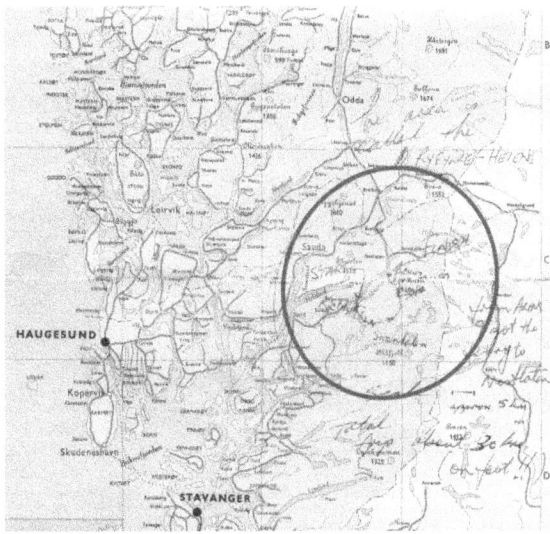

My fantastic hike thru' the Norwegian Mountains
The area is called the RYFYLKE-HEIENE
From Arhus I got the ferry to Nestlaten.
Total trip about 30 km (on foot!!)

**Notepad entries while in the Norwegian mountain country near Strandalen.**

It's frustrating travelling through country like this knowing that there is no satisfactory way of recording its grandeur. A photograph would never show the depth of vision or the enormity of distance and, even if a painter could capture the mood, it would be technically impossible to record the infinite detail.

Neither can I rely on my memory to recall the country in its entirety. Of course, I can attempt to recall the sights. The mountain ranges disappearing in gigantic folds to the horizon, or a mountain peak towering into a turbulent crown of cloud, or the aqua-blue lake water, still and deep, under an overhang of ice, or the blinding white light that throws into your face as you sludge across a snowdrift.

And the sounds – the effervescent bubbling of the mountain

streams, the scratching of your boots across the loose stones, or the occasional chirp of a bird when you're not too high. Or the most incredible sound, when you're out of earshot of the streams and birds, and you stop the shuffling of your feet, hold your breath, and become enveloped in the deathly quiet cloak of pure silence.

All of these I can recall individually to adequately savour, but my memory fails when I try to combine them and recall the country and its impact in its completeness. Probably the best way I can attempt to recall these mountains is to remember the sensation — when you stop and take a slow 360° turn absorbing the beauty and the power and feel the energy of this magnificent land focus on you from the awesome peaks above you and the crystal water below you, and mainly from the enormous distances around you, feeling all this power, beauty and energy focused on the relatively tiny point that is you.

Tiny you stands at the focal point of all this energy and you absorb it all and feel yourself grow huge and become one with it all.

<u>The next day, out of the mostel.</u>

Descending now, already below the tree line, the mountains move slightly apart to form a deep ravine for me to pass through, with a river falling down the middle to show me the way. The country has changed, mellowed. There is no stark light anymore — it's filtered through the cool trees. The water is no longer icy blue but becomes clear green when it takes a rest on the rock pools before re-joining the white foam and continuing its race to the valley.

Leaving the ravine, and gazing down into the deep valley below me, I can see the lake reflecting the greens, whites, and greys of the mountains opposite and the pale blue of the clear sky. It's beautiful of course, but a placid beauty, and I prefer the spectacular stark beauty of the higher country.

*At Lake Suldalsvatnet (near Bratveit)*

*The first glimpses of the farmhouses at Bratveit tell me I'm back in civilisation, though I'm still a long way from the twentieth century. A pleasant stroll down through barns, cows, dogs, and sleepy old ladies, then I'm at the jetty on the lake waiting for the ferry. As I look back along the shore of the lake at the mountains stretching straight up out of the water and miles back into the wild country I've just crossed I have two feelings – one of accomplishment and one of regret for my journey's end.*

In my contemporaneous notepad entry, I allude to an instant of self-consciousness while I was on that mountain peak: a focal point of energy; becoming "one with it all". Decades later I attempted to expand on my abstruse reaction.

### MY MOMENT ON TOP OF THE MOUNTAIN

I clambered onto the peak, lifted my eyes, and scanned that massive imposing panorama; it enveloped me. And then something strange happened; I still consider it my most spiritual experience.

All that vast magnificent volume, in an uber-conscious instant, seemed to expand to some limitless beyond. And I was abstractly aware of being its focus: I was its centre – I felt overwhelmingly and ecstatically *included*.

It was a sublime sensation. I've since tried to rationalise it; but without much success: maybe it was a spark of so-called 'cosmic consciousness'. I certainly wouldn't try to interpret it in any traditional religious sense with a god or gods and suchlike – I don't believe there was any omniscient divine intelligence involved. Whatever it was, it was utterly elating; even if fleeting; and incomprehensible.

Maybe it happened because I hadn't seen anything like that landscape before: my Western Australian home state is renowned for its flatness. Or maybe I was just fatigued, lacking oxygen. But it doesn't especially matter to me 'why', it just 'was' – and it didn't require anyone's prophets: sacred or secular.

I've never had the same feeling since, at least not that intensely. It didn't seem as synthetic as some drug-induced rush. Closer perhaps would be those concentrated moments of affinity-with-nature – but amplified; or maybe an extraordinarily passionate moment of 'joie de vivre' – but this felt much more acute.

I still wonder about it once in a while: was it a flicker of enlightenment; novice nirvana? But it wasn't anything to do with dogma or ritual – I didn't practice either. It seemed to me to be somewhere between sensory and cognitive – or maybe both together: perhaps where emotions might dwell.

I didn't have any imperative interest in replicating that instant; I was too busy exploring the tangible world. And in the intervening decades I really haven't had the urge either, and probably for the same reason: the tangible world is endlessly interesting. But I'm glad I experienced that moment. I think it gave me an idea of what spirituality might be – or what I expect spirituality should be.

**A silly story I wrote while waiting for the ferry at Suldalsvatnet.**

<u>Why I Hate Clouds</u>
(or another reason why me and the Sun are buddies)

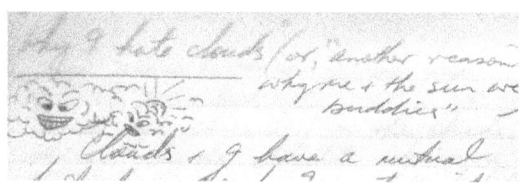

Clouds and I have a mutual hatred. Though I must point out Clouds started it. I have never provoked a Cloud and, as a matter of fact, there isn't much I can do to a Cloud anyway – except hate it.

For reasons known only to them, Clouds take pleasure in harassing me. When I pay large sums of money to visit a lookout tower, or when I spend hours of gruelling time climbing a mountain to see an 'incomparable view', Clouds surround me and all I see is the grinning faces of my old arch-enemies.

When I gather my courage and dive into cold water in the hope that I will soon dry in the warm Sun, I surface only to find that a Cloud has raced across miles of sky to block the heat and I end up shivering in the shade while Clouds chuckle above me. When I'm trying to hitchhike and I find myself miles from the next shelter, with no immediate hope of a ride, Clouds enjoy adding insult to injury by massing over me and inviting their friend Rain to come and help make my life a misery. There have even been times when Clouds, in particularly nasty moods, have also invited Thunder and Lightning to join in the fun.

There are rare occasions that I take pleasure in Clouds by sorting out pictures from their otherwise formless shapes, like faces or ghosts or, on really good days, maybe a map of the world. But when I try to point out my artistic discoveries to my friends, Clouds instantly rearrange themselves into their usual shapeless selves just to make me look silly.

This brings me to "another reason why me and the Sun are buddies". The good ol' Sun hates Clouds too because Clouds love to join up and block the good old Sun's view of the good ol' Earth.

However, the good ol' Sun is almost as powerless as me when it comes to getting rid of Clouds — the biggest Clouds anyway. What the good ol' Sun can do though is dry up the little Clouds that stray too far from the main groups. If the good ol' Sun didn't do this then all the little Clouds would soon become big Clouds, then there would be no stopping them running the whole sky. That's why I can't help but give a little chuckle when I see a little Cloud trying to block the good ol' Sun by itself. In only a few minutes the good ol' Sun dries it up into nothing and then comes beaming through to give me the good ol' buddy wink.

It's nice having a friend in high places.

**29 JUL 1975**

I got a bus out to Haukeli. There are no cars out here except the occasional holidaymaker. I figure I'll bus down to Kristiansand then a ferry to Denmark to hitch to England. A *five-hour bus ride through fabulous scenery (which is starting to annoy me — it's so incredible that you just let it pass you by after a while). Cliffs hundreds of feet high and sheer into crystal clear lakes with trout jumping out of the water, rapids, pine trees, wildflowers — insane! I get to Kristiansand and the ferry to Denmark is 100 kroner!*

Nearly AUD30 at the time; or my weekly travel budget for a single fare.

*It's big decision time, worse than in Stockholm — which way to go?*

**30 JUL 1975**

*I reserved my ferry seat for Harwich then checked around for buses, share costs, or anything to get over the channel and into England — but nothing.*

I calculated it was likely better value to get a ferry from Kristiansand direct to England. Although it was a lot more expensive than the Denmark ferry, it wouldn't require hitchhiking down through northern Europe again, so less time and consequent cost. And I would save on a night's accommodation as it was an overnight ferry crossing.

After I reserved a seat on the Harwich ferry, I investigated a Newcastle alternative. I also checked if there were any other options to reduce the fare: sometimes there were packages where you could join a bus trip that included a cheaper ferry fare; or you may find somebody crossing with their car and you could share the fare as a passenger. But I didn't find either option.

*Also, nothing much in Kristiansand so I spent most of my time in the library.*

**30/07/1975**
**Postcard from Byglandsfjord, Norway**

*Hi, This is the type of country I just took a three-day hike through with a Norwegian nature freak I met. We stayed up there for*

two nights in log cabins. On the second day we left our packs on the trail and climbed the highest peak in the area. It was a fabulous experience and I saw the most beautiful country so far. There's much more to tell but no room. I got the sad news about Nan a few days ago. A bit of a shock. Give my sympathies to Pa and Mum. I'm on my way south now, back to GB and Scotland and Ireland. I've got a Norwegian surprise I'll send home from there.

Love to all,

sure-footed Jeff.

My "Norwegian surprise" was my copy of the Sorlandet newspaper in which I featured. I found out later that my ever-hopeful mother surmised my surprise might be an announcement of my meeting and partnering with a Norwegian girl. She was disappointed – me too.

**31 JUL 1975**

Big decision – the Harwich ferry is cheaper than to Newcastle, so I bought it. About $50 for one night over while sitting up in a seat. It's leaving tomorrow. Back to the library to wait.

**1 AUG 1975**

I escaped from the camping ground without paying and managed to save about five dollars (a small win at least). The ferry left at 2PM. Uneventful. I read 'Khrushchev' and went to bed (my seat). Already everything is cheaper.

Where I got the ferry to Harwich (London).
Also the place where I made headlines.

**2 AUG 1975**

Arrived in Harwich. Jolly old England. I hitched easily to

London. I got the underground to Victoria Station to get some money. Really exciting. The station was packed with people hustling and bustling. I'm the only one smiling. It's nice to be back. My old Vicarage Gate room price from February has gone up but it's still cheaper than the YMCA. Glen lives down the road. I went to see him. He's going out to a disco, so I'll see him tomorrow.

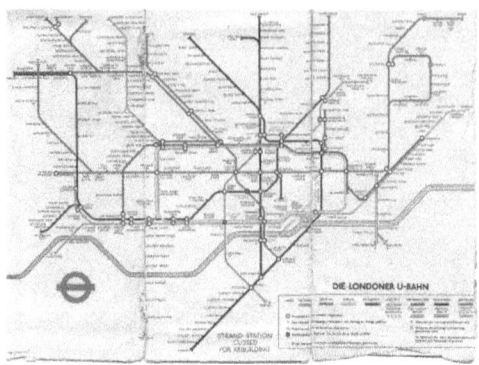

There were only German copies left

Glen was a fellow passenger on the S.S. Ellinis who stayed in London after disembarking to work and save money before travelling, as a few did.

I rang the folks – a 9 minute phone call!!!

International phone calls were not cheap. I made this call from a phone box; reverse charges most likely.

**3 AUG 1975**

London is very hot! A quiet Sunday. I strolled around familiar areas. I hung around home, watched TV. I went and saw Glen in the afternoon, and then over to his friend Rob's place. Then we went for some Turkish food and went to 'The Hoop' pub for a few beers and tried to make conversation.

**4 AUG 1975 to 10 AUG 1975**

Again, I can't keep a diary in London. I went and saw The Who's 'Tommy' movie – not much (Eric Clapton was playing a stringless guitar). Also saw Bernardo Bertolucci's 'Last Tango in Paris" – a great story but the ending was bitter. I liked Marlon Brando's passion. I visited the British museum – it

> didn't excite me much. The Science Museum though is great. The English queue philosophy is still going strong, but the Latin tourists bust it up.

For a long time, there has been a notion that the English like to queue, and I do recall being impressed with the orderly queuing that I saw around London. But it was also apparent the southern European visitors had no such predilection.

I was amused by the contemptuous 'tut-tutting' of the Londoners as the 'Continentals', oblivious of the 'rules', would barge to the front. It had only been a few years since Britain had joined the European Union (better known then as 'The Common Market') and maybe the English were still a bit apprehensive of 'Johnny Foreigner'.

> Also, the newspapers haven't changed — still pathetic human-interest stuff. London is nice in the sunshine, though it can't take the heat. I went to Petticoat Lane looking for cheap stuff, but it's a huge tourist rip-off. Prices are higher than in the shops. I went to a pub in the East End where Teddy Boys are still going about — really weird. Pink socks, combed pushbacks, DB's, monkey suits. I'm drinking a pint of cool Black Label Lager at the moment. A great beer — meaty stuff. The other night I heard a chick in the 'Old Swan' pub call Foster's Lager "that fizzy stuff".

**11 AUG 1975**
> Checked-out of my room and went to pick up my mail. It's not there yet so back to Vicarage Gate. The old bag charged me the new arrival rate. I spent the afternoon back at the Science Museum — a great place (the pendulum guy closing up shop, ha ha).

In the foyer of the Science Museum was a huge Foucault pendulum hanging from the ceiling three floors above. It very slowly oscillated, and its wide swing plane appeared to steadily rotate clockwise around the room. But the swing plane was actually fixed, and its apparent rotation was demonstrating the rotation of the Earth.

## England

People stood around in fascinated contemplation when, at closing time, the doorman shuffled a cradle over to the pendulum bob and unceremoniously dumped the heavy ball into the cradle, thus bringing a sudden stop to the machinations of the universe and snapping us all back to the prosaic realities of life.

### 12 AUG 1975

I phoned WA House, and my letter has arrived. I packed up and went to get it. Most of day was getting the ring insurance fixed up. I finally jumped a green bus out to Wycombe. It's nice being back in the countryside. I started hitching and got a truck lift out to Oxford. I could have gone on to Manchester, but it was getting dark and I'm too tired. Oxford is very English – a cop on a pushbike.

### 12/08/1975
### Letter from Oxford, England (very)

Hi!

Just got your letter today. Thanks for the hostel card, as soon as I hung up the phone the other night I remembered it. Also got the insurance thing for my opal ring fixed up at Aussie house (by the High Commission JP himself). I just got the money all fixed up into 740 American dollar traveller's cheques. Very nice being rich again! On rough calculation changing $600 Aussie into $740 American, I lost about $60 American. I checked it out with the bank but it's all legal. The exchange rates don't you know. I missed John by less than a week. Still, I may run into him somewhere.

My Norwegian surprise is the newspaper. It's a southern district-type newspaper – see if you find anything interesting – like bottom left front page. It's all very nice but not completely accurate – still a nice souvenir.

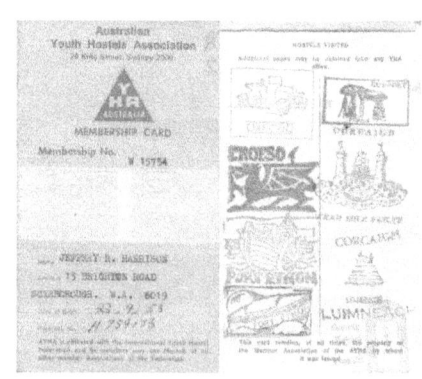

London was nice for a while but it's pretty easy to get fed up with the hustle and bustle. It's much nicer out here. It's the England you see in the movies – all very English. I got directions to this hostel by asking a bobby who was cycling down Jack Straw's Lane about late afternoon teatime. It was pretty hard to keep from laughing while I was talking to him.

There's a rock festival near here on the 22nd so I'm going over to Ireland and will try and make it back here for it. Groups like Yes, Hawkwind, Robin Trower, Wishbone Ash, and some others. It's a three-day camping thing, I'm not sure what it'll be like, but I've never been to one before, so I'll try to get there.

This was the 15th Reading Jazz Blues & Rock Festival. Also featured were Judas Priest, Dr Feelgood, Thin Lizzy, Ozark Mountain Daredevils, Supertramp, Joan Armatrading, Caravan, Soft Machine, Mahavishnu Orchestra, and many others. But I didn't get there, I was in Dublin on the 22nd; it might have been a memorable introduction to a rock festival!

I've checked out the Asia trip from here and it seems okay so it's still on.

Happy birthday Mum! xxx

See you (relatively) soon,

Jeffrey (plain old Jeff just doesn't do in Oxford old boy)

## 13 AUG 1975

I headed out of Oxford. One lift with two chicks and a guy. Me and a very beautiful chick on the backseat. I mentally did indecent things to her. Later I got fouled up on the motorway near Gloucester, then finally a long truck ride to Swansea with a Welsh guy – I hardly understood a word he said, I just put in a few "yeh's" when it seemed right. Also, a lift with a Pakistani guy who brought up the embarrassing 'White Australia Policy' again.

The infamous racist Australian immigration rules known historically as the 'White Australia Policy' were designed to prevent people of non-European ethnic origin from immigrating to Australia. It came up uncomfortably often in my conversations with drivers and others. Initially I was mostly unaware of its reputation, but many people I met explained how widely offensive it was.

As they enlightened me, I could only offer my ashamed deference.

> I got a bus to Port Eynon youth hostel. Very touristy and booked out – so I pitched the tent.

**14 AUG 1975**

> Three guys from the hostel offered to give me a lift on one of their motorbikes. A great lift through the country 'Easy Riding' it. Me on the back of the leading bike with two others either side and to the back. We tore up the road. Then a fast ride in a Ford Capri to Cardigan where I hung around, waiting for the rain to stop, and for a bus to the youth hostel in Newport.

'Easy Rider' was a 1969 cult movie that featured two young men touring the USA on motorbikes. A Ford Capri was a sporty fastback coupe of the era.

> The youth hostel is full of schoolkids – pity, I was looking forward to a quiet Welsh night – ha ha.

**Diary Note:**

> I was very sad today (August 14, Wales). I realised that my adventure is nearing an end. I thought back to life at home – no getting up in the morning, hitting the road, and sleeping where I end up. I think the best part of this sort of travelling is the freedom.

**15 AUG 1975**

> I woke to the sound of screaming kids. Then a nice walk down the hill along a winding cottage-lined lane. One of those flashes of super happiness. I got a lift to the ferry and spent most of the day either on the ferry or waiting for it. I got to Ireland

and then a train from the port to town and into a camping area just as it got dark. A nice position on a small beach cliff overlooking the bay with town lit-up across the river. A kid helped me with my tent. PS: I was hassled at Irish Customs – they thought I was a junkie – ha ha.

**16 AUG 1975**

The day started well with two big truckloads of racing pigeons giving me a send-off. But by 4PM I was only 15 miles from where I left. I finally got a half decent ride to Waterford where I decided on a bus to Cork. Arrived at 8PM and made it to the hostel. I took a stroll and had a dinner of chicken, chips and Guinness, which tastes better in Ireland. I hope hitching improves.

**17 AUG 1975**

I hung around Cork for a day. I went out to Blarney Castle and kissed the stone. American tourists can be funny (not funny ha ha). The best part was 'Rock Close' nearby. A very spooky little area – a good place for leprechauns. Cork is filthy and Catholicism is rampant (generally true for all Ireland on both accounts). A lot of poverty also.

Ireland in the 1970s was not the economic 'Celtic Tiger' of the late 20th and early 21st centuries. It was also culturally conservative; Catholicism was dominant and widely influential.

Yet people are still very cheerful and friendly (except towards hitchhikers).

**18 AUG 1975**

I headed out for Limerick and got a lift straight off with a woman and two kids. A nice lady who bought me a Guinness and gave me a pack of Rothmans. She left me a few miles out of Killarney after talking me into going there. I started on my way and from there everything went shit-house. I got one more short lift, got a bus for a pound, missed Killarney, and ended up 20 miles past at Tralee. I tried hitchhiking in the dark, but no good, I went back to the train station and slept on a bench. I woke up in the middle of the night getting wet from rain.

**19 AUG 1975**

I got the train into Killarney. A much nicer area then the rest of Ireland. Pretty country. I bought a ticket for a bus tour of the Ring of Kerry. Never again, it was piss weak — people saying stuff like "look at that rock", and a guy taking pictures of anything. Also, a guide pointing out stupid things — like a bolt factory. I got back to town and checked into a bed and breakfast. I went to the pub and knocked back a few Guinness.

**20 AUG 1975**

I spent 4½ hours on the exit road from Killarney. I finally got a ride out to the next town. I spent most of the day on the road. Then into Limerick at last — another filthy town. The hostel is disgusting. But I feel sorry for the old guy running it on his own. 'Porridge fever' hostel is very funny.

A shabby old man was trying to run the hostel by himself; he didn't seem to be coping, or he was beyond caring. It was all pretty filthy but there was a jovial mood among the lodgers. A porridge-themed running joke had been enthusiastically continued for an evidently long time; contributions were on all the notice boards and graffitied throughout the building.

I played chess, first time in ages. I've lost a lot of imagination — I played a gruelling game.

**21 AUG 1975**

The day started well, I got a lift straight off to the next town with a social worker. We got a reasonable discussion going. He was interested in Oriental crime rates, but I didn't really know

> what he meant. I then got stuck on the road for next few hours and finally got a lift all the way to Dublin. I checked into the hostel. Dublin looks okay so far. I had a bit of a splurge and had grilled rainbow trout for dinner. I drifted back to Bunbury.

*O'Connor St, Dublin*

A few years earlier I worked for a short time in the regional town of Bunbury in Western Australia. I lived in a motel on a travel allowance, and relatively luxuriously. I dined in the restaurant each evening on extravagant meals like rainbow trout.

**22 AUG 1975**

> I had a look at Dublin. Trinity is more or less how I pictured it from JP Donleavy, but I didn't think it would be so central.

*Trinity College*

JP Donleavy was an Irish-American author. I had read several of his books; some were based in Dublin and Trinity College which awarded him an honorary doctorate in 2016.

> I bought a Liverpool ferry ticket and then just walked around generally and stumbled onto the modern art museum. I realised that a lot of modern art is shit.

Hopefully my art knowledge and appreciation has matured over the decades, but I can still have problems with a few modern art movements: some geometric abstractions and colour field paintings seem cold and perfunctory. My dilettante's view of painting is that it's a visual medium and so, primarily, I want a painting to be satisfying when I look at it, without too much intermediate cerebral analysis: I want 'a feast for my eyes'.

I accept contemporary art must push against boundaries; there is always space for theory and allegory. And I recognise the 'feast' idea is attributed to Eugène Delacroix: a Romantic painter from 200 years ago. But, for me, initially my experience of a painting is sensuous – I want my eyes excited before my brain tries to interpret what I'm seeing.

> I'm still seeing a lot of poverty in Ireland. I had an interesting discussion with a 67-year-old tramp guy in the street. He was just busting to talk serious with someone, so I obliged – we didn't get anywhere, but it was fun.

**23 AUG 1975**
> I left my backpack at the bus station and walked over to Phoenix Park via the Castle and City Hall. This is the real lousy part of town – even the park was shit-house. Cattle are left to graze on the lawns so there's cow-shit everywhere. I spent the afternoon in a cinema watching heavily censored movies. I got down to the ferry and sacked down on the boat deck – I slept well on a cardboard box.

**24 AUG 1975**
> The ferry landed at Liverpool, and it was deserted – a bank holiday weekend. I headed for the bus station while singing Beatles songs. I caught a 'Magical Mystery Tour' to Blackpool. The whole city is just one big sideshow of amusement arcades. I decide to stay overnight and check it out. I found a cheap camping place and went into town later at night. It was exciting at first, but it got boring and depressing later on. A dumb place for a holiday.

**25 AUG 1975**
> Tried to get to Edinburgh but I left it too late. I got flooded out last night. Little puddles in my tent. A lousy hitching day

England - Scotland

*– only two lifts – I ended up getting a bus into Carlisle at 8PM. It's beautiful English countryside up here near the Lake District. I checked into the youth hostel and played chess again against a club member. A 10 minute game – I lost but not disgraced.*

**26 AUG 1975**

*I walked up to a roundabout and an exit of the M6. It was like hitchhiking in the Indianapolis 500.*

The M6 Motorway runs south-north from west-central England to the Scottish border. It's a very busy major artery with three lanes both ways.

*Finally, I got short lifts to the middle of nowhere then a truck lift to the middle of nowhere again. Then a good lift to Edinburgh. The guy (Henry) offered to take me back to London too – on Thursday. Edinburgh is really beautiful. I bought a ticket for the Tattoo tomorrow night, then I came down with the flu and crashed in my YMCA room.*

**27 AUG 1975**

*Edinburgh WOW! A magnificent city, and the Festival is in full swing.*

Each August the Edinburgh Festival Fringe takes place simultaneously with the Edinburgh International Festival to become the world's largest arts festival. Included is The Edinburgh Military Tattoo: an annual series of musical and marching displays performed by military bands from

*Edinburgh looking down Princes Gardens*

British, Commonwealth, and international armed forces. It takes place at night in the magnificent setting of the Esplanade in front of Edinburgh Castle.

> The Castle is the best I've seen. Then to a free rock concert in Princes Gardens, then up to Calton Hill and a view of the city, bay, and sky. Then a free open-air play. Then just wandering around the beautiful old city until the Tattoo started. The Tattoo was a spectacular show. I enjoyed every minute – a fabulous atmosphere – singing and clapping. There were Aussie police in the pipes and drums. I went to see it as a 'necessary sight' but enjoyed it as a spectacular and great show.

### 28 AUG 1975

> Got a train to Slateford then moseyed up to the auction room to meet Henry. I just caught him, then we were on our way to London.

I had arranged to meet Henry at an auction room he was attending (two days earlier he had kindly offered to drive me to London).

> We stopped at a Royal Air Force base and had to check in at security. A very long drive down super roads through the ugly Midlands. I'm excited being on the last leg of the trip. Henry dropped me off at a train station. I said thank you and got a tube to Earls Court (tsk tsk).

## London

Earls Court was a notorious London hang-out for ex-patriot Australians. It was widely considered a bit provincial to stay there, and there did seem to be a large representation of 'ocker' Australians.

> I checked into low-cost accommodation then went for dinner, I came back and watched TV, then I went to go to bed but seven people were on the floor of Room 3 so I tried Room 4. But I caught two naked folk in the middle of the floor doing what comes naturally – "Oops sorry". I scurried back to make eight people on the floor in Room 3 (while a bit jealously green around the edges).

**28/08/1975**
**Postcard from Edinburgh, Scotland**

Hi!
Just a note to let you know what is happening. I left London and went through Oxford, Wales, to Ireland, from Killarney up to Dublin, then over to Liverpool and Blackpool, and up to Edinburgh.
Edinburgh is fantastic! I saw the Military Tattoo and the pipes & drums were from Aussie police forces. A magnificent show – really spectacular. I'm on my way back to London

now and I'll be there tonight. I'm thinking of getting a bus straight to Munich and then start heading home.

I'm excited to be heading homeward and sad to be ending the trip (though I've still got a lot ahead). Overall (at the moment anyway) I feel damn tired! But it's nice thinking back to what I've seen and done.

See ya soon,

McJeff

PS: in London now (29/8/75) and leaving by 'Magic Bus' at 7PM.

NOT TOO SOON EITHER, BLOODY IRA ARE AT IT AGAIN!

On 28th August 1975 a bomb exploded in Oxford Street, London

## 29 AUG 1975

I bought a ticket for the Magic Bus to Munich.

The Magic Bus was a loosely managed company that capitalised on the 'Hippie Trail' traffic.

Since the mid-1950s Western travellers had wandered along a freely defined overland route between Europe and South Asia, mainly through Iran, Afghanistan, Pakistan, India, and Nepal. In the 1960s the route became increasingly popular with the hippie sub-culture and those mostly younger travellers looking to travel cheaply, lightly, and spontaneously, and to mix more closely with the exotic (and newly trendy) local people: it became known as the 'Hippie Trail'.

Many of the hippies were also interested in 'pot' and other recreational drugs that were freely available along most of the journey. In the late 1970s political upheavals in Iran, Afghanistan, and Pakistan brought an end to the 'Trail'.

The Magic Bus acted more as a booking agency than a coach fleet company. The buses were often independently owner-operated. The vehicles could range from reasonably modern, high-back seated Mercedes to dilapidated old Bedford-style, straight-back seated jalopies. In my experience the buses were more likely to be the former west of

Istanbul and more likely the latter to the east. They picked up travellers

in London, Amsterdam, and Istanbul and travelled through to Kabul, Kathmandu, and Delhi (and returned – sometimes). The routes and timetables were flexible and often determined by impulsive majority decisions by the twenty or so passengers.

*I spent the day trying to get a cholera shot. No bastard would do it. So, at 7PM I got on the Magic Bus down to the ferry. The prick driver wouldn't let me get my sleeping bag out of the bus, so I froze to death on the ship and didn't sleep at all well. I'm not impressed by Magic Bus so far.*

**30 AUG 1975**

*Somewhere in Holland we shuffled onto another bus and a few hours later we were in Amsterdam. I checked out head office for the right departure time then went back to H88 for a shower. I never thought I'd see Amsterdam again. It's a better crowd on this big tourist bus. It's about 30 years old with music and much nicer than the other one. I slept on-and-off and we stopped now and then for coffee and eats.*

**31 AUG 1975**

*We arrived in Munich at 6AM. They let us off the bus just out of town. I met up with two guys, one North Irish (Dermot) the other English (Clive), and we got a tram into town.*

These giant music boxes are everywhere (Amsterdam)

At one time I casually remarked it was "funny" that, if Dermot and Clive weren't travelling Europe together, they might have been on opposite sides of a current deadly conflict (i.e., Northern Ireland and the 'Troubles').

They both sternly rebuked me, saying there was nothing at all "funny" about it, and they had friends and family who were directly affected. I quickly learnt not to comment further on that serious affair, of which I was fundamentally ignorant.

> They stayed at a hotel, but I moved into a campsite. I slept from 10AM to 3PM and was woken up by a brass band floating down the river. Guys were surfing in rapids.

There was a narrow and fast flowing channel exiting the river. It created a stationary wave that a group of young guys were surfing on mats and belly boards.

> I went into town to meet Dermot and Clive to go to the Hofbräuhaus. I drank 4 litres of beer and got drunk on an empty stomach. We wandered around town and went to a brothel, but I didn't buy. I got the subway home somehow.

**1 SEP 1975**
> I woke up with a stinking hangover. I met some Aussies up at the shop at brekkie. Also, a city of New Zealanders surrounded me last night.

A tour bus of New Zealanders had arrived and pitched their tents all around mine.

> I had to meet the guys at 12 o'clock to go to the brewery. I went into town and then went out to Dachau. Not a nice place to visit. I went back to town and met the guys. We walked uptown to the State of Mind area and had a few quiet beers and a lot of conversation.

'State of Mind' was Munich's famous Schwabing bohemian quarter. In the 1960s and 1970s Schwabing became an internationally renowned party district with legendary clubs and bars.

> A nice night — we talked politics, women, and dope. Then we

said our goodbyes – they're going on to Salzburg.

**2 SEP 1975**

I woke late and strolled around town. A very big town and spread out. Big solid buildings with big plain statues on them – very German. Then out to the Olympic City.

Munich hosted the 1972 Summer Olympic Games.

Fantastic! All plexiglass and cables hanging from big poles in the ground. It was like a big tarpaulin – I shook the main stadium roof!

I could access and swing on one of the steel cables supporting the acrylic glass roof and it seemed to me that I was causing the enormous structure to move – a little bit.

I headed back into town and managed to down a hamburger, chips and two milkshakes. I finally broke my fast but not on the best food.

**3 SEP 1975**

I moved half-heartedly out of Munich. I didn't feel like hitching again, it's been a while since I last did, and I've got soft. But every time I'd go to get the train I'd get a lift, so I finally got to Innsbruck. The last lift was a beaut. A young German kid who just didn't know how to drive. He scared the shit out of me on alpine roads in a powerless VW. We nearly had a head-on crash. I was glad to get out, he reckoned he was going to Rome – ha ha! The Alps just spring up out of the plain, and spring a long way up.

**4 SEP 1975**

> After a lot of ballsing around I finally found the youth hostel last night. Today I checked out Innsbruck. Not very impressed. Maybe I'm getting too hard to please, but it's too expensive and not as picturesque as I'd have liked. The gold roofed balcony (Goldenes Dach) was nice and so are the other buildings in the old town. The hostel is a club for local teenagers too. Very loud as usual with these folk — I was glad to move on.

**5 SEP 1975**

> Hitched out of Austria okay. Nice being back in Italy with cafes and an easier way of life. I got a lift with a nice Italian couple who spoke German (Torins?)

"Torins" was probably my mishearing of "Tyrol" or "Tyrolese", a Bavarian dialect spoken in northern Italy. South Tyrol, a region in the Alps, is another of many European curiosities. It was historically within the Austro-Hungarian Empire for centuries up until the end of WW1 when it was seized by the Kingdom of Italy. So, although a part of Italy, the native language of most of the population is German.

> Then a lift in Trento with a homo wearing undies who blew me a kiss. I got a train from there to Venice. Great first impression — I took a boat trip down a lit-up canal and there were singing gondoliers. The youth hostel was closed so I spent the night in an expensive place with a dormitory and a nude chick in the next bunk. These beautiful women are making me crazy.

**6 SEP 1975**

> I booked into the youth hostel, then I checked my backpack into

> the train station and checked out Venice. A great city – it's very different. I like the little alleyways – it's like walking in a maze. Some streets are dead ends into the canals – no cars! I catch a number five boat to the train station. Still not very cheap – because there's lots of tourists of course. I checked into the hostel after a big hassle in the queue. "We haven't changed – our hair is longer".

"We haven't changed…" is a reference to something I'd read about the failure of the 'peace-and-love' hippie ideal to fundamentally change peoples' attitudes. My diary entry was a reflection on a display of aggression amongst the young fellow travellers queuing for the youth hostel.

> There's a big Communist rally here now. I don't think the Soviets would approve.

The rally had a distinctive Italian flavour – music, singing, and a general bonhomie. It seemed to be more a festival than a rally.

**7 SEP 1975**

> I met up with Fernando from the Communist rally last night and we went out to Murano to buy some glass. Great stuff out there but the good stuff was too expensive. We watched some glass blowing. Back to town and there was a parade down

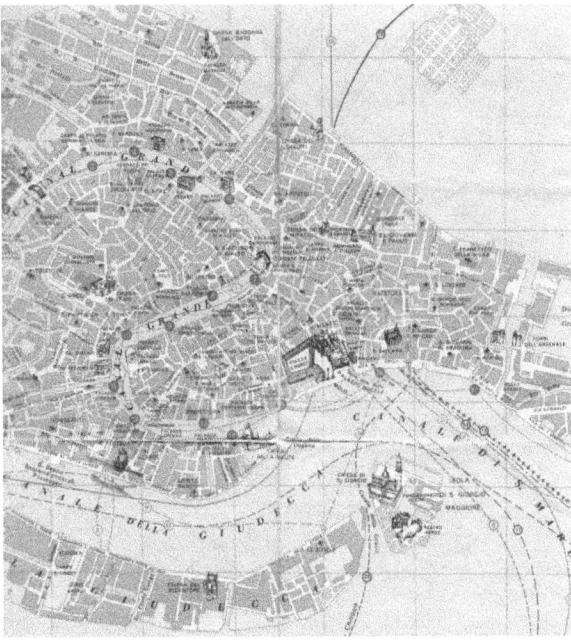

Canal Grande. Afterwards we wandered into the 'Royal Box' – no one stopped us. Then we had a good discussion about everything. Fernando is a very concerned guy and committed against the USA. Back at the youth hostel I got into the commie rally with Mexicans, Italians, and Germans – all commies, and me in the middle – "Yay! Viva la comunismo!" – ha ha.

I was mostly apolitical at the time or concerned more with specific issues that may have directly affected me rather than any general political philosophy. But my personal politics now are certainly progressive and humanistic: so left-of-centre. It's very likely I began to develop my social democratic leanings during my travels in 1975; possibly initially influenced by my experiences at this rally.

**8/09/1975**
**Postcard from Venice, Italy**

Hi,
I think I last wrote from Edinburgh – moving right along I'm now in Venice and heading for Yugoslavia. Venice is great, just as you'd expect. I'm sitting at the station now waiting for a boat to take me down the canal. There are no cars or buses

> in Venice. Crazy little alleyways and canals. Munich was ok, the best part was the Olympic Stadium. I got drunk at the Hofbrauhaus with an English guy and an Irish guy drinking litre steins of beer. I've already picked out a Greek island to have a holiday from my holiday. I might take a couple of weeks to just eat, sleep, swim, and hang out in the sun. Write to me in Istanbul.
> Ciao, Jeffioni.

**8 SEP 1975**

> I spent the whole day on trains – super lazy. I changed route through Yugoslavia to include Belgrade. I had an insane conversation with an old commie in Trieste station. He was telling me that "the Australian government are fascist for not supplying roads in the Simpson Desert". My first impression of Yugoslavia is not good.

Back then the Federal People's Republic of Yugoslavia was a single country made up of the now independent countries of Croatia, Bosnia and Herzegovina, Serbia, Montenegro, Kosovo, and North Macedonia. It had a communist government with Marshal Tito as President for Life.

The little I saw of the country wasn't inspiring. Compared to the countries I'd visited previously it seemed poor and grim with a lot of high-rise dull grey concrete buildings.

> I got ripped off at the station, put on the wrong train, and was hustled for a hotel at Zagreb (shades of Morocco). I spent the night in a youth hostel full of giggling girls. I'm thinking of going to Sophia in Bulgaria.

**A notepad entry on the Communist at Trieste Station**

> Then there was the guy in the station at Trieste who had an unbelievable argument as to why the Australian government is not a peoples' government but a capitalist government. He said – "I read there were four people who died trying to cross Australia driving from north-west to south-east in a car. They died because there was no road. Yet the Australian

*government can afford to send troops to Vietnam but can't afford to build roads".*

*Another gem was that the aim of communism was to abolish money. "What will replace it", I asked. "The people will work in a factory then get a card. Then they can buy what they want with the card. Everybody will have all they want with no money – simple. By the way – people are only happy when they are working, preferably in a factory".*

There was a small map of Australia on the inside cover of my diary. I used it to try explaining to him the vastness and hostile environment of much of the Australian continent, and the consequent unreality of building roads in that specific area. But he was only familiar with European geography 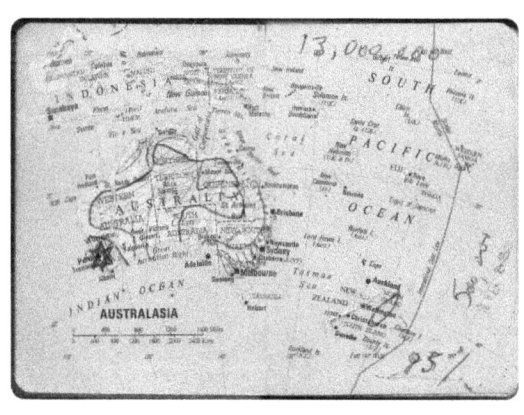 and population densities, so I couldn't convince him.

In his favour though, he did seem to prophesy credit cards and debit cards! But I still doubt all factory workers are happy.

**9 SEP 1975**

*My first ride was to 100 km out of Zagreb, then the second ride was from a Greek guy going to Thessaloniki, so forget Bulgaria. The whole day spent in a car. Yugoslavia is a very drab place to look at. We nearly got wiped-off again near the border. One car was last seen running off the road.*

In the 1970s many Greek nationals worked in Germany. Consequently, there were seasonal holiday exoduses to visit families in Greece. The route traversed Yugoslavia and the driving was reckless. There were frequent roadside memorials; several times I saw cars, inside long tunnels, or blind mountain bends, overtake by crossing into oncoming traffic lanes.

*We picked up a Berliner couple on the border. Later three of* us had dinner together and talked about our expectations of "paradiso" Greece. Then we looked for somewhere in the street to bed down. We were woken an hour later by a train passing within 15 feet.

We had unrolled our sleeping bags and bedded down on the side of the street; we hadn't noticed a railway crossing very nearby. Waking up at ground level to a moving freight train just a few feet away was very scary.

Then a dog was barking at us, then rain. At about 4AM we were looking for another sleeping place in a garage and a local caught the Berlin guy in his undies – very funny. I slept on a cafe steps – "it won't open till 9AM".

**10 SEP 1975**

The cafe opened at 6AM and woke me up – less than three hours sleep! I left the German couple still asleep and got a train to Bolos. I walked around and got an exorbitant quote for a hotel, nothing else here, dead tired, so I decide to get the train to Athens and sleep on the way. I slept on-and-off and arrived about 12 midnight. Found a room for 60 drachmas in a brothel-type place reminiscent of Morocco. I realise I probably won't hitchhike again now until Australia. I'm not particularly sorry after the last few rides. I had a shower and collapsed on a rock-hard bed, but I could have slept standing up.

**11 SEP 1975**

I got up and decide it's no fun sleeping in a sewer, so I went looking for somewhere else. I found 'world-famous Diana's' and booked into their cheapest space on the roof for 30 drachma's a night. A good place – very funny signs everywhere ('no hanky-panky'). I checked out the Acropolis. Athens is in a setting that reminded me of Ghardaia in Algeria. Very hot and dry. The Old Town is fabulous (e.g., houses under the Acropolis).

Athens has advantages of Europe and Africa – a good place. I bought sandals at a flea market with me doing all the hassling for a change. I snuck into a tour at the Acropolis and apparently it was a lot more in its day than is now (e.g., the statues were painted).

Had a good cheap dinner at a restaurant – my first food in a while.

**12 SEP 1975**

I slept well on the roof. Had brekkie first and then got my cholera shot (at

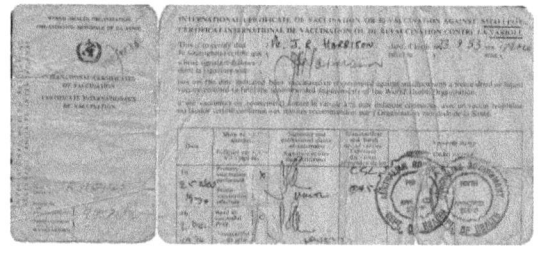

last). I sat in a park and wrote a letter then wandered into town to get a ticket for a 'Light & Sound' show and arrange my islands trip. I did neither but checked out Agora (old Athens). I spent the day just wandering around, then went to the 'Light & Sound' display (a French production, typically overdramatised).

The 'Light & Sound' display was a summer night-time attraction where the floodlit Acropolis and Parthenon were viewed from about 1 km away on Pnyx Hill. There was an accompanying historical commentary. I only half enjoyed it. It was spectacular but I thought it was a bit too chintzy and formulaic.

Then I went for a wander through the nightclub area. I went

into one club to see a 'Fascinating Light Show' and had one beer for 50 drachmas! I should have known better.

**A notepad scribble – a song or poem:**
## 'The Athens Disco, I Should Have Known Better'

I should have known better than to come in here
with the goodtime girls and the triple-price beer.
It was just to see the 'Fascinating Light Show'
and it's not as if I really didn't know,
I didn't know better.

Well they sat me down and they brought me a glass
and it wasn't too long before a girl made a pass.
We talked for a minute then as quick as a wink
she asked me if I'd like to buy her a drink.
I said I'm sorry girl but I'll have to let you know
I just came in to see the 'Fascinating Light Show'.
When she saw I didn't have any money to spend
she gave me a shrug and got up and went.
Another came along for a "dance and nothing else".
I said no thank you please I'm just sitting by myself.
Then another tried to take me over to the corner.
I had to think for a bit before I didn't think I oughta.
I said I'm sure I would find it would be very nice
but I really don't know if I could afford the price.

I should have known better than to come in here
with the goodtime girls and the triple-price beer.
I wanted to see the 'Fascinating Light Show'
but it's not as if I really didn't know,
I didn't know better.

I finished my drink and the show was no thrill
so I moved to the bar to fix up the bill.
I said how much do I owe for a very small beer?
He said only 50 drachma is what we charge here.
I spat and I swore but what could I do,

so I paid the man and made a move.
The girls hissed me out but I wasn't at all bitter,
I just walked out the door saying —

I should have known better than to come in here
with the goodtime girls and the triple-price beer.
I just wanted to see the 'Fascinating Light Show'
and it's not as if I really didn't know,
I didn't know better.

–ooOoo–

**12/09/1975**
**Letter from Athens, Greece**

Hi!

I was going to send a postcard, but I thought I'd tell you about Greece and there's no room on a postcard. I haven't got to the islands yet, and I've only really seen Athens, but if it's any indication of the rest of Greece, then the islands must be paradise.

Athens itself is too nice to be a capital city. It's stinking hot and sunny. I'm staying at a youth guesthouse and sleeping on the roof with a whole lot of other travelling types for 75 cents a night ("showers included but no hanky-panky"). The food is the best part — and cheap. Last night I really splurged and spent two dollars and had a cheese salad and a big hunk of veal with spuds drenched in olive oil. For lunch I'll probably stop at one of the little delis that sell big meat, cheese & tomato rolls (grilled) for about 25 cents. You can buy fruit in the street really cheap too. I just had a big fresh apple for a couple of cents. I don't know what prices in Aussie are like now but, compared to the rest of Europe, Greece is very cheap — cheaper than Spain.

The city is in a valley surrounded by big dry limestone hills and Athens is sort of an oasis. The Acropolis is in the middle on a big hill and, now and then, you can see it down the end of a street. The people are beautiful. Those that speak

English will come over and help you out in the shops or on the buses. The waiters and barmen enjoy trying out their English and the young waiters serve you with big grins and want to know where you're from and where you're going — a really nice atmosphere.

A lot of the talk at the hostel is about the islands, people either coming or going to them. I've decided on Santorini. Apparently there's a beach there where a lot of people have pitched tents and a little hippie freak community has built up. I'm going down there in a few days and I'm going to sleep, swim, sunbake, more sleep, and eat lots of food — generally get super healthy for Asia. I'm looking forward to the rest.

I think I wrote last in Edinburgh. I got down to London in one lift then got a bus to Munich. I spent a few days at Munich the best part being the Olympic Stadium — like a giant perspex tarpaulin. I also got very drunk at the Hofbräuhaus drinking litre steins with an English guy and an Irish guy. After Munich I got down to Venice which was really nice — just like the postcards and movies — all little winding canals and gondoliers and such. I bought two postcards and wrote one but forgot to send it. Then I went into Yugoslavia and luckily got a lift straight through to Greece. From my first impression of Yugoslavia, it was very poor but, unlike Greece or Spain, has no class. The people weren't too groovy either — at least the ones I met.

I've got to a stage where I couldn't be bothered with a country if I'm not going to enjoy it. I've had enough of experiences no-matter-whether-enjoyable-or-educational-but-hell.   Now I'm looking for good times. I've talked to a few people about the Asia trip and, as I expected, the Middle East countries are not a barrel of laughs. So, I probably won't break the trip from Istanbul to Delhi but get through the Middle East with a nice bus window between me and them. "I just couldn't handle the hassles, man".

By the way, everyone so far that I talk to has used more money on the Asia trip than I've got. I won't be staying as long as a lot of them did but be prepared to answer any desperate screams from around Singapore way. I imagine there are good communications between Singapore and Perth. How about a letter in Istanbul — I should be there in three or four weeks.

Agapi,

Jeffapalapagossolinki

**13 SEP 1975**

I got my typhoid shot in my other arm so now both arms are useless. I got a bus out to Sounio to see the Temple of Poseidon. Not very spectacular. The best part was the little green bays on the coast with swimmers and such. American tourists are really getting under my skin today. I hope Greece can persevere.

A few American tourists I came across were conspicuously over-demanding and over-loud.

I got back to town and had a souvlaki dinner and went to bed not feeling too good with no arms.

**14 SEP 1975**

I left the roof about 6AM and got down to Piraeus for the ferry to Naxos.

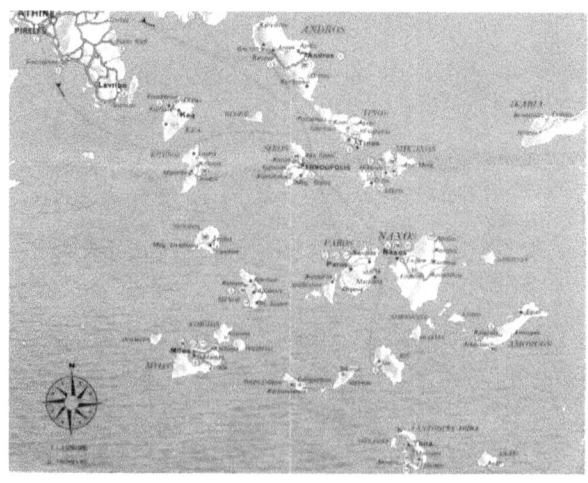

> I was on board with two minutes to spare. An uneventful cruise, it didn't seem to take long. We were in Naxos about 3PM after a stop in Siros. The Paradise Bus to Apollonas cost 70 drachmas so bugger that, I'll sleep on the local beach tonight and get the ferry to Thira tomorrow. It's not what I was expecting here, it's like Sorrento Beach but with stronger winds.

Sorrento Beach in the north-western suburbs of Perth was, back then, a featureless beach with a frequent strong afternoon sea-breeze. So, my diary description sarcastically attests to how especially windy and sparse the Naxos beach was.

> It's scenic though – mountains, white villages, beach bars. I got nostalgic over Simon and Garfunkel music playing at the bar, then I went to bed.

**15 SEP 1975**

> I headed into Naxos to get the ferry to Thira at 4PM. I had a swim to fill in time. I was hanging around town when a bus pulls up and asks me if I'm going to Apollonas. "Ok" says me, and then a crowded and scary bus ride across the island on winding mountainous roads. The mountains are very dry and dotted with white villages. We got to Apollonas. A nice little village – three tavernas and a church, a small wharf, and a little swimming beach and surf beach. I met Mark, a German-English guy. Everyone else here is German. Cheap food and drink, I played backgammon and drank retsina.

The retsina we were served in the tavernas was a coarse white wine with a distinctive pine resin flavour; we were told it was uniquely Greek and historically ancient. Although it took a few glasses to acquire a taste we quaffed it by the bottle; it seemed authentic, and it was very cheap.

**16 SEP 1975**

A New Zealand chick took us to another beach today. All the nudists are here. A nice setting with a little bay and freshwater stream in the middle. We tried some fishing and caught three small rock fish. After fishing I just hung around the beach reading and sunbathing surrounded by nude women. I did a bit of rock-climbing then went back to town and had dinner and more retsina, then back to our beach camp just round the bay a few hundred metres from the village to hear some beautiful music with two guitars and a flute, just jamming in the moonlight.

**17 SEP 1975**

I slept late then went to the taverna for brekkie and backgammon, then went to try fishing with Mark but no good. Back to town and I body-surfed at the beach near the taverna. Only little wind waves but I caught a few rides — a lot of fun. I just hung around a bit more playing backgammon and fishing. I had a dinner of squid, eggplant, and a few bottles of retsina and stayed up till midnight playing backgammon with a German guy.

**18 SEP 1975**

I intended to get the 10AM bus to Naxos but no bus till 4PM. So, I sat around eating, drinking and playing backgammon with Mark. We decided on a swim. A chick asked us if we'd like to share a taxi to Naxos for the bus price — "ok". A nice drive down a new road through beautiful country — a bit like Morocco. Music and chicks in the back seat. We got into Naxos and sat around eating and drinking waiting for the ferry. Then a rough passage to Syros and a bus to Vari Beach for the night.

A real shitty place. Very built up with a 'castle' on the point and post stamp sized beach.

**Diary Note:**
Sitting on a little man-made beach at Naxos watching the old people bobbing along in two feet of water thinking they are swimming, then trying exercises on the beach like waving their arms madly about in any direction they might go. It's depressing. I really hope I can stick to a physical fitness program through life and not try to regain shape when it's too late, because it looks like it's impossible.

**19 SEP 1975**

We bussed back to Ermoupolis and got money at last and did a bit of shopping — melons, hot dogs. A very picturesque bootmaker mended Mark's sandals. Watching him work was like looking at a 17th century painting. Then we got a bus to Galissa. Not much here, we had a swim then we found a cave and moved in. We tried some fishing but the wind really shitting everything up. I had

a great taverna dinner of stuffed tomatoes and a few drinks. The place got crowded with a jukebox with one Beatles record, and Greek music with some old guys dancing.

Mark and I were joined by a handful of young tourists in this very modest and remote taverna.

After a while several local men wandered in and, while drinking liberally, they became more and more convivial – especially towards the couple of girls in our group.

Some of us fed the jukebox to amplify the jovial mood. The locals were less keen on the solitary Beatles record but, after they persuaded us to select some Greek music, they began to dance 'Zorba' style: solo in a cleared space between the tables with fingers clicking and arms swinging. Their dancing became a sprightly joyous contest; it was a laughter-filled fun night.

**20 SEP 1975**

We had brekkie and got a bus back to Ermoupolis. We waited till 8PM for the ferry to Samos. We generally just hung around town. I tried some fishing off the wharf. The ferry came in and we both got through with one ticket — a half price trip. There was a very strong wind out at sea. I slept on-and-off on the deck — I struggled to stay on my seat in the wind.

**21 SEP 1975**

We arrived in Samos at 5:30AM and still dark. We found the youth hostel and I crashed till 10AM. Woke and seemed as though I had spent a couple of days here. I met an Aussie guy who's just come from Asia. I spent the afternoon on the roof eating fetta, tomatoes and bread and talking about Asia with him. Then I moved into town for a drink and a wander. I got back to the youth hostel and there were a few new arrivals. We hung around and played chess then we all moved off for dinner and the movies. Movies were not on till next month, so we went for a drink and more Asia talk.

**22 SEP 1975**

I got a bus to Kokkari. Really nice country. I decided to walk on and look for a beach near the cemetery. Some guys stayed, four of us went on. We found a great little set-up with mountains, a bay, a nice beach, and a taverna right on the water — it's all modernised, but nice people. The taverna chick is from Sydney and speaks with a Yankee accent. A taverna guy gave me some calamari and I tried fishing. I spent the night playing cards and drinking, and then back to the beach in bright moonlight for a sleep.

## 23 SEP 1975

Woke up — my birthday! The guys sang happy birthday at breakfast. I picked flowers for our taverna table. I just stayed around near the taverna all day — reading, playing chess, sunbathing, rock skimming, fishing. Late arvo I caught one fish and an octopus. I took them back to the taverna and they cooked them for our dinner. I had a big meal and a few beers all treated for my birthday. Then we joined a couple of tables together and some Dutch people came over for a party. They gave me pickled herring and cigars. We stayed up till 2:30AM singing old Beatles songs and drinking.

## 24 SEP 1975

Went for breakfast about 11AM. Played some chess and read till 4PM then me and Brian took a hike up to the mountains to a village. We found an ancient road shortcut straight up the hill crossing vineyards and a stream. We arrived at a spotless untouched village, all painted purples, oranges, and greens and beautiful. We had a lemonade in the square where all the men were gathered for cards and a fast Greek version of backgammon called tavli. We took the longer mountain road back to the beach.

## 25 SEP 1975

After a morning swim I went into the taverna for brekkie. Played chess and finally finished HG Wells book 'The Shape of Things to Come' — 500 pages took a long time to read. I got a bus back to Samos at 4PM. I checked into the youth hostel and did some washing. Brian and the three Germans arrived, and we went down and booked tickets for the boat to Turkey, then we went back to a taverna for a drink and goodbyes to Mark, then had a big dinner and went to the movies with Kung Fu and Clint Eastwood.

## 25/09/1975
## Postcard from Samos, Greece

Hi!

Off to Turkey tomorrow to start the big Asia trip. I've been beach bumming around the Greek islands for a couple of weeks now. Staying at a beach about 16 km from this place for a few days just swimming, fishing, and eating real good cheap food.

Had a birthday party there with a group of German, Dutch, and Swiss friends. I got presents of flowers, fish, and cigars. A nice party. Happy birthday to Dad too.

$500 left to get home but I should make it, it's getting cheaper all the time. Hope there is a letter for me in Istanbul. Look up Samos in the atlas, it's near the Turkish coast south of Izmir. We get a little launch in the morning across the strait.

See ya soon, salty brown Jeff

## 26 SEP 1975

I was up in time and got a very small slow boat to Kusadasi (Turkey). First impression is a nice mixture of east and west – all the cheapness without too much pressure. I got a bus out to Ephesus and wasted 10 lira seeing more rocks.

I remember it being a hot day, and

Ephesus, Turkey between Kudasi & Izmir. Saw it with Brian and the German guys

Turkey

the ancient ruins of Ephesus being spread over a large area and with limited shade. Also, this late in my adventure, I was probably becoming a bit blasé and unappreciative of the value of what I was seeing.

> I then went on to Izmir. I found a student hostel and had hassles with a "lost" German guy.

My memory of this episode is also "lost".

> I scored some hash, but it was no good. The food is shit-house after Greece, so is the sanitation.

**27 SEP 1975**

> I woke up with sores all over me. I thought it was bedbugs. Had brekkie then split up with Brian and the guys.

*Izmir, Turkey.*
*Walked around here looking for a bus to bus depot for Bursa*

> I found the tourist bureau and got all sorts of information and decided on Bursa. After a long bus ride, I arrived at 'another town'. I decided to stay overnight then push on to Istanbul and get a move on. Now I think the sores are an allergy, there are too many for bedbugs. They're a bit like I had in Ghardaia.

**28 SEP 1975**

> Up late and had a shitty brekkie. I'm not eating too well mainly because the food turns me off. I got a bus into Istanbul. The old town looked good from

*Sultanahmet, Istanbul*

177

> the other side of the Bosphorus with silhouettes of mosques. I found a hotel between Eminonu and Sultanahmet. There's plenty of freaks in town.

"Freaks" was another term for the hippie travellers. Istanbul was a main staging point of the Hippie Trail and almost all travellers on their version of the Trail went through Istanbul.

> The locals seem to be used to travellers. The town is not as picturesque as I'd hoped.

**29 SEP 1975**

> I went to the Pudding Shop for breakfast. So-called hippies all getting ripped off on self-service food.

The Pudding Shop was the common name for the Lale Restaurant in Sultanahmet. It became popular in the 1960s as a meeting place for travellers on the Hippie Trail. But it seemed to me, in 1975, to be trading more on reputation than authenticity.

> I checked out the Magic Bus to Kabul and visa stuff, then I went to see the Blue Mosque. It was more impressive from outside than inside, pretty interesting anyway. Then on to the Grand Bazaar.

*The Grand Bazaar*

> Not bad but not as good as the Moroccan medinas. I generally just ballsed around the old town, knocking back deals and

dodging spit and shit on the road. Everyone wants to buy my watch. I can handle these guys so far, maybe because of my experiences in Morocco – I know what to expect now.

**30 SEP 1975**

I did a boat trip on the Bosphorus on the public ferry. Really cheap and a nice little cruise. A very busy harbour. The bridge is over half a mile long, we went under it. I went to buy food on the boat, but cockroaches swarmed out onto the counter. Back in town I checked into the youth hostel for a shower.

## Part III – Downhill to Home

Since arriving in Greece, when I knew my hitchhiking was over, I felt a bit like I was now beginning an easier 'holiday'. I made a mangled attempt at explaining my change in attitude when I wrote to my parents from Athens: "I've had enough of experiences no-matter-whether-enjoyable-or-educational-but-hell. Now I'm looking for good times".

And they were good times in Greece, especially the Islands, and now I was getting on a Magic Bus for a journey of just over three weeks. Travelling by bus would require less effort: it would be a relief not needing to hassle for transport to my next day's destination; accommodation would often be left for others to organise; and I'd be sharing adventures with new friends for longer than the usual episodes of just a few days. What I didn't foresee, but probably had an inkling of, was the amount of drug-facilitated partying that would ensue.

Recreational drug culture in the 1970s was pervasive. Just a few years earlier the hippies of the 1960s associated marijuana use with the widespread anti-establishment response fomented by the Vietnam War protest movement; there were 'Legalise Pot' rallies worldwide. Contemporary literature was awash with drugs references: the celebrated poet Allen Ginsberg was an advocate for marijuana; the psychedelics guru Timothy Leary famously wanted us to "turn on, tune in, drop out"; avant-garde writers Hunter S. Thomson and William S. Burroughs painted anarchic drug-drenched literary pictures; and dog-eared copies of Carlos Castaneda's 'The Teachings of Don Juan' stood on countless brick and pine-plank bookshelves. And within popular culture: few parties were without a request to play Bob Marley's or Cheech & Chong's cannabis themed albums; anarchic underground press like 'International Times' and 'Oz' included drug use in their spheres of counter-culture interest; in the smash hit movie 'Easy Rider' Peter Fonda, Dennis Hopper, and Jack Nicholson made drugs 'really cool'.

So, as similarly aged and culturally aligned passengers on our Magic Bus from Istanbul, we knew we were likely heading into a smorgasbord of world-renowned hashish and other psychotropics. But, looking back now, I'm surprised at the intensity of our consumption, and the rate it continued after we left the bus.

I bought a set of visa photos in Istanbul in late September. They were necessary for the visa applications I would need while crossing through Asia. I can remember being unhappy with the photographer here, and I think it shows. He was charging me an exorbitant fee and I was unable to find an alternate option. I was aware that I needed to look predominantly conservative for my Asian visa applications, so it's instructive that the photo shows my presentable best at the time. This photo is  probably the most 'respectable' I would look until more than three months later when I settled back into suburban Perth.

After leaving the bus everything was supposed to continue in holiday-mode. Subsequent transport, accommodation, and general living costs were reputedly very inexpensive and easy to negotiate all the way through the subcontinent and down through Southeast Asia to home. But, of course, expectations are not always realised. As events transpired, I was on the bus a bit longer than I'd anticipated and, even after leaving it, some friends, the drugs, and the partying continued. My enjoyment of alcoholic inebriation transferred readily and easily to the endemic narcotics.

But, even through that effected haze, I still discovered a trove of geographical, cultural, historical, architectural, and artistic treasures.

## 1 OCT 1975

I went to the Topkapi Palace for a taste of the old Sultans' life. The Treasury is better than any I'd seen in Europe (fist sized emeralds, a precious coral buckle). I checked out of the hostel and picked up my passport from the Iranian embassy and, after running all over town trying to cash money, I finally got on the Magic Bus for Kabul. First night and all the hash came out and we all got stoned and slept on the bus.

Topkapi Palace, Istanbul

## 2 OCT 1975

We got into Ankara about 5AM and off the bus for a few hours to get food and money. I can't remember what happened in between but arrived at Sivas and I went and had dinner with Don from Sydney and some English guys. I went back and slept on the bus in the street.

## 3 OCT 1975

We woke up with people all around the bus. I met three nice chicks who took me away and bought me brekkie, then later they bought me a biro and cigarette holder.

Three lovely Turkish school students were fascinated by us on the bus. They were also keen to practice their English. The biro and cigarette holder were an elaborately hand-decorated and tasselled set I used, and cherished, long afterwards.

We were back on the road in the desert when suddenly, we were in the snow. Some deadly roads then we arrived at Erzurum. We grabbed a bite to eat, played some backgammon, and then hit the bus.

## 4 OCT 1975

*We ballsed around in town for most of the day getting a compressor fixed. People were going crazy peering into the bus — a travelling circus show. We finally hit the road, only went a few kilometres, and then stopped at a roadside cafe for dinner and a few beers. We decide to stay overnight and had a bit of a party and slept on the tables. I helped the owners clean up and they gave me free tea.*

## 5 OCT 1975

*We got going and, on the way, we passed Mount Ararat. A beautiful snow-capped mountain just sticking up out of the desert. Where Noah's Ark is somebody said? Got to the border and heard some great music by an old guy on a drum and a young guy on flute. Also, a bit of dancing by the locals. We went right through the night on the bus.*

## 6 OCT 1975

Tehran, Iran. – Shahyad Aryamehr Monument

*We got into Tehran and went to a hotel, but it was too expensive, so we all agreed to go up to a dam in some hills outside of the city and camp out. We took everyone but the Greek.*

"…everyone but the Greek": I don't recall the significance of this, but it's an intriguing sentence.

*We bought meat, spuds and beer and found a place near a creek and lit a big fire. We ate roasted meat and potatoes then*

# Iran

sat around the fire and drank and got to chatting and general partying

**7 OCT 1975**

A great day. I woke up and did some clothes washing in the stream then, when the sun hit the water, I had a wash and a swim. I was body surfing the rapids when crowds of locals started arriving and gave the chicks a hard time.

We were swimming half-naked, including the girls. It must have been disconcerting for the culturally conservative local Iranians. And we were in an area a considerable distance from the usual travellers' route.

We started smoking Russian hash out of bottlenecks.

We made some rough chillums (a simple conical smoking pipe) from broken bottles. Using a chillum was a bit of a performance but also an extremely effective way to inhale a lot of smoke. The technique involved cupping your hands together with the chillum protruding through your entwined fingers. You drew the smoke through the space created between your thumbs. A damp rag was wrapped around the base of the chillum and across your thumbs to make a seal and to cool the smoke. You needed a partner to fire the contents while you drew on the chillum.

I got really stoned and took an inner tube down the rapids. We later went down the road to a café for a big meal then on our way for an all-night drive to Mashhad.

**8 OCT 1975**

We stopped in a small town for a break and wandered around the shops and little street-front factories – coppersmith, blacksmith, carpet makers, and carpenters – all hundreds of years old. Then we arrived at Mashhad and got into a nice

*Campsite, Mashhad*

campground with tents and beds and showers. We went by five rial taxi to town and got some money and walked around a pretty dull town. Then went for a kebab dinner and seven of us got picked up by a guy who took us to his turquoise shop.

Turquoise is a blue-hued semi-precious gemstone. Historically it has been sought after as Persian turquoise and there was an abundance of shops and jewellery makers selling it.

I traded my army hat and a cheap chain necklace for four turquoises.

Beautiful mosaics
Real gold

### A Mosque in Mashhad

A guy took me and Dave down here for a look thru the gates (only Muslims allowed inside) then he took us to a Persian carpet shop and back to the Afghani Embassy.

All these guys are commission blokes but worth a free cup of tea & free taxi service & guide service. A lot of fun letting them hassle you while you play tourist.

**9 OCT 1975**

I went with Dave to get my visa. The carpet guy picked us up and took us to the consulate for free then took us to a beautiful gold domed Mosque with mosaics, then to a Persian carpet factory. Fabulous carpets — very tempting to put down a $30 deposit. I got the visa then went back to the campground and had a

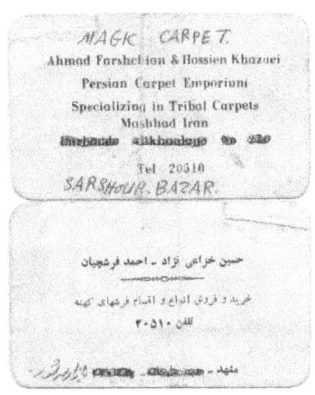

smoke with some Norwegian guys in their tent. Played a spot of Euchre then hit the sack.

**10 OCT 1975**

We were on our way after picking up a few more passengers and got to the Iran border in the afternoon. We spent the whole day at customs and police offices trying to get into Afghanistan. After all sorts of red tape, we finally got refused permission because the bus isn't insured. We must stay at the border overnight. Had dinner and free tea at a restaurant owned by an English-speaking Afghani. Then we hit the bus for sleep. There was a lot of funny ballsing around on the bus.

**11 OCT 1975**

We were into Herat early. I scored a deal while the rest of the bus was at the bank. We checked into a hotel and walked around trying to buy clothes. Good stuff here but they say hold on until Kabul. We went back to the hotel and got a little party going and got very stoned and went out to a restaurant for eggs and chips and I was hassled for some reason by the little manager guy.

**12 OCT 1975**

We left early after a smoke or two, then on the bus we dropped some opium and a few hash balls.

We'd been on the bus for twelve days; over 3,600 hot kilometres from Istanbul to Herat. Our naturally ventilated Magic Bus had hard straight-backed seats and only a few of them were vacant. During almost the whole journey there was at least one passenger, often the most seriously afflicted by gastric problems, prone on the floor or sometimes in the overhead open luggage racks.

We washed on the limited occasions we were able to. The road from Herat to Kabul was especially harsh; flat and dry; there were few scenic distractions. Eating opium or hash was not only beneficial in relieving tummy-rumblings and other physical discomforts; the catatonic effect was also useful when you leaned your head on the rattling bus window

## Afghanistan

and disappeared into your own spiralling thoughts as the road-miles laboured past.

> We just cruised all day past Sahara-like country. One time it was just sandhills to the horizon. We got into Kandahar just at dark and had a good meal of vegetable stew and chips. I got a big rush off eating and collapsed in the bus for a sit up sleep to Kabul.

**13 OCT 1975**

> Got into Kabul and booked into Koochi Hotel near Chicken Street.

Kabul's Chicken Street was a famous general meeting place for travellers on the Hippie Trail. It was in an area with cheap accommodation, restaurants, and shopping.

**14 OCT 1975 to 18 OCT 1975 – Blank Pages in Kabul:**

On **13 OCT 1975** I make a one-line entry in my diary recording our arrival into Kabul. The next five pages are blank. On **19 OCT 1975** I begin my diary entry with "I woke up sick…"

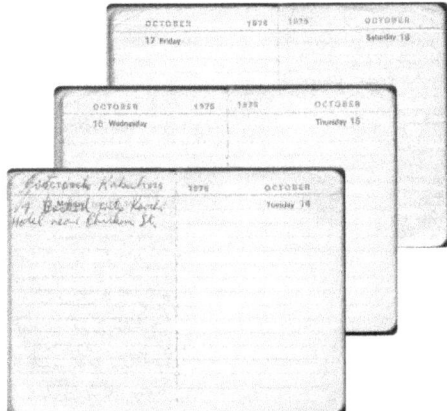

I don't have a solid recollection of what happened in those unrecorded days. I remember the famed black Afghani hashish was easily procurable. And I still have an impression of the almost Biblical aspect of Kabul.

There were only sporadic signs of western influence, otherwise the streets, shops, and people looked as they probably did hundreds of years before. An enduring memory is the butchers' shops. There was no refrigeration; carcases were displayed hanging from racks open to the street front; there were a lot of flies.

A clue to what happened during that interval is in my **28/10/1975 Aerogramme from Delhi, India** where I mention the Magic Bus stayed in Kabul for a week. I can also vaguely remember us partying in Chicken Street, and an occasion when, forgetting our usual cautious avoidance of eating meat, we succumbed to the temptation of hamburgers. Not a prudent decision given the standard of the butchers' shops, and possibly why the first entry I make in my diary after the blank pages is: "I woke up sick..."

**19 OCT 1975**

*I woke up sick, and didn't eat all day, but spewed, shivered, and shat all day. At about three o'clock I decide it's time for hospital. I've got gastroenteritis. The hospital is out of the Middle Ages. They shot intravenous into me, and flies licked up the blood spills. I shit in a bucket near the bed then later in some construction site outside, in the middle of the freezing night.*

**20 OCT 1975**

*A miserable night followed by a breakfast of stale bread and cold tea. I tried to leave but they wouldn't let me go until 10:30AM. The bus was leaving at 11AM. I finally escaped and got into town, but the bus was at the hospital to pick me up. I finally re-joined them, and we headed for Pakistan. We went through some really deep gorges and came out at a shitty town before the border – too late to go through the border so we camped outside of town. I had a can of Kraft cheese from Melbourne for dinner for one dollar.*

### A NIGHT IN HOSPITAL IN KABUL

The walls were rough plaster and the ceiling had exposed rough-sawn log beams. An intravenous drip was snatched from an open shelf and carelessly administered by a grubby, bearded nurse. He made several attempts at piercing my arm before succeeding. There were traces of faeces on the bed, perhaps from the previous patient. I was alone in the ward, which was just a room with a few beds with small side cabinets; there was no call button.

I passed a horrific night; I shivered from fever and cold. I soon filled the bucket at my bedside, and I couldn't see a bathroom or toilet, or recognise any direction to any. In desperation I dragged my IV stand outside into what seemed to be a building extension in progress; I squatted in the bitterly cold darkness. By the morning I felt much better and, appraising my situation, I determined to leave – but first I needed a doctor's permission. It was reluctantly granted after my insistent pleadings, and I headed back to Chicken Street.

My experience of 'third-world' medicine was sobering for somebody who took 'first-world' conditions for granted, but I appreciated the Afghani medicos had freely provided me with health care (and saline solution) and nursed me back to a fit-for-travel state – especially when their resources were so limited.

Back in Chicken Street I found some of our bus passengers. They were waiting for the bus to return from the hospital with the others – they'd gone to check on me. I had only bought a Magic Bus ticket from Istanbul to Kabul; the bus might have justifiably continued onto Pakistan without me. I was still quite ill; it would have been difficult to navigate on from Kabul by myself. After a short while we all reunited and headed off for the border.

Their decision to collect me, and extend my passage on to Delhi, was a rescue amid my adventure for which I remain extremely grateful.

## 21 OCT 1975

*I slept really well and washed in a creek – feeling a lot better. We got to the Afghani border but were stuck there for hours getting through, then we were into Pakistan. It's a bit better than Afghanistan already. Guns are everywhere and a lot of activity. Then through the Khyber Pass. A few gun shops but not much more.*

We were anticipating the infamous and purportedly lawless Khyber Pass; and it was an eye-opener. I remember a lot of guns; either for sale or just casually carried; all a bit off-putting, so most of us stayed mostly on the bus. I saw antiquated rifles, modern machine guns, and one weapon that looked to me like a bazooka.

*Then Peshawar. We had a meal in a very clean restaurant then booked into the rooftop at a hotel. Peshawar is all in English and with coloured lights.*

Pakistan was still somewhat poor by standards west of and including Iran, but it instantly seemed centuries ahead of Afghanistan. Of course, it was immediately much easier for us with the universal English language. My "coloured lights" referenced the improved available facilities for us as travellers.

**22 OCT 1975**

> We hung around waiting in Peshawar all morning. Some of us took a horse and pony ride, ate ice creams, and played snooker while waiting to leave.

I don't recall why we were delayed in Peshawar, but we were often delayed. There were various reasons: bus maintenance; some travel or customs requirement; waiting for access to money or fuel; or sometimes an individual health problem – like me in the hospital in Kabul.

> We got underway through some lush country. We crossed a wide river over an old army bridge with a huge fort built into a hilltop on the opposite side.

The river was the Indus, and the fort was Attock; both significant landmarks we were not cognizant of on our Magic Bus trip (as my diary entry attests). I don't recall seeing anybody, other than our driver's sidekick, refer to a map or guidebook; illustrating our journey was essentially a passage and not a tour.

> We stopped for some bus repairs and went for a drink at a country club bar (maybe military – also tennis courts, swimming pool etc.). We stopped for the night on the side of the road after attracting a big crowd at a food stop. Customs police live in a haystack here.

We recognised these Pakistani Police as Customs; we'd seen the same faded uniforms when we crossed over from Afghanistan. But we didn't discover why they were in this remote area far from a border; they may have been on some temporary mission. They had set themselves up with makeshift beds and cooking kit alongside a dishevelled haystack.

They were a friendly and jovial lot; perhaps we were a welcome and novel distraction from their assignment.

**23 OCT 1975**

> We slept on a sandhill. The police made us a cup of tea for breakfast (some guys also got straight-edge razor shaves). I took a ride on a trolley up a railway line across a bridge. The bus got away after a while. We stopped in Lahore for a bit. I talked to a student who was already married at 19, earns $9 a month, and is learning English at school. We met up with another bus at the border and raced through the Pakistan side but were 10 minutes late for the Indian side, so we got stuck in no-man's land for the night. A nice dinner, played cards, and crashed in the customs house.

**24 OCT 1975**

> After a few more border hassles we got into India – after a very thorough check. We stopped at Amritsar and saw the Golden Temple. I shopped around and bought fireworks and vegetables for 3 rupee (16 cents). Some really cheap souvenirs too. I drank lots of choc milk. Me and Wayne took a rickshaw to buy some beer – an insane ride, flat out through the crowds, sitting back and swigging beer from a bottle. We camped out in a pot garden and had another party.

*Golden Temple, Amritsar, India*

We had stopped off the main road to camp overnight in a patch of forest. As we were settling down for the night some passengers wandered around the bus perimeter and explored our immediate surroundings. After a short while one of the Americans rushed back excitedly holding a handful of a green shrub – "wild pot!"

Some of us being less knowledgeable asked – "what makes you think its pot?" I remember his emphatic and disdainful reply – "I *know* it is". Why there was a mini-forest of cannabis there was a mystery to us, but we harvested too much of it anyway and proceeded to party.

We had whole plants hanging upside down from the luggage racks inside the bus. The following few days we merrily trialled different samples as they were passed up and down the aisle.

### 25 OCT 1975

> Brian got into a fight last night and spoiled the mood. We got underway and just cruised along in the bus all day with our luggage rack stash. Everybody feeling good and ignoring Jill and Brian.

Brian was our lone bus driver: a burly Midlands Englishman. He occasionally had an aggressive tendency but, in retrospect, he must have had a difficult and worryingly responsible task – especially trying to herd us lot, and in the condition we were usually in. Jill was Brian's Australian girlfriend and the bus 'stewardess' and general organizer.

> Everyone else just grooving along. We passed our first elephant. Delhi is big and modern in parts. We arrived at night and found a hotel and had ham steak and pineapple for dinner.

### 26 OCT 1975

> Everything was closed for Sunday, so we went into Connaught Place for coffee and breakfast. We stayed there for the morning and later met everybody at the bus, then went back to the hotel. I had a real good club sandwich for dinner then we grabbed two Harley taxis and went to the circus. Some acts were

a bit weak but generally it was okay.

"Harley taxis" were three-wheeled rickshaws built on WWII surplus Harley Davidson motorcycles; they could carry up to eight passengers.

**27 OCT 1975**

> Breakfast again at India Coffee House – a great place and cheap. I sorted out some cheques at American Express then down to the Nepalese embassy for my visa. I checked out flights. It works out cheaper Delhi-Kathmandu-Bangkok. Then I checked out a jewellery shop. Really nice and cheap stuff but I can't find a stone I like. Phil bought $50 worth. I had a great Chinese meal and hit the sack.

It's possible my diary entries in India, and their focus on 'what I had for dinner', reflect my enjoyment since Pakistan, but especially in India, of the excellent food quality (and commonplace refrigeration). I may also have been more focussed on what I ate after my gastroenteritis episode in Kabul. Or, as other diary entries prior to Kabul suggest, my obsession with my dinner may have just been a common trait for any twenty-one-year-old male.

**28 OCT 1975**

> We went on a city tour. New Delhi is big and spacious, but the sites weren't much. The best part was the Buddhist temple. We got back to town and had a chicken dinner then got blown away in the bus. We went back to our room and scored our own deal. We got more blown away again and went to the movies. Saw 'Khartoum' – a really shitty movie.

**28/10/1975**
**Aerogramme from Delhi, India**

> Hi!
> Sorry I haven't written for such a long time (I can't remember when I wrote last) but all sorts of places have gone by in the last few weeks, and I just haven't got around to it. I got a bus from Istanbul to Kabul and the people were okay and they stayed in Kabul for a week, so I stayed on the bus to here. It

took 3½ weeks and, except for going through Pakistan a bit too fast, it was pretty good.

I'm perfectly healthy now, and the worst of it is over, but in Kabul I spent a night in hospital with gastroenteritis (a real weird experience). India is pretty nice, and it looks as though it's going to be cheaper to fly from here to Kathmandu, then on to Bangkok, than to fly from Delhi to Bangkok. So maybe I'm in for a few flights soon. I should arrive in Bangkok with $200 so maybe I'll get home on what I've got.

The route now is Delhi – Kathmandu – Bangkok – Penang – Sumatra – Bali – Australia. I'll keep going as far as I can and, if I run out of money, I'll have to get you to send me a flight ticket. I'm buying all sorts of junk on the way, and I may buy a new ring in Bangkok. Delhi is a relief after Afghanistan. It's a nice cross between modern facilities and super cheap prices.

I'm staying at a hotel with a group of guys from the bus and we're having a lot of fun living like kings in this town. Still I'm looking forward to getting into Thailand and the south-east countries where it's supposed to be a lot nicer and more interesting. Jewellery is cheap here and in Bangkok, so is silk and carved wood and clothes. There's all sorts of stones like topaz, sapphire, amethyst, and you can have them set in gold or silver into anything you like.

How about writing to me in Bangkok care of American Express and placing a few orders so I know what to buy for presents – plenty of good looking jewellery here but I'm not sure what everyone would like. Also, if you can send me the current Aussie prices of gold and silver per ounce, it might be worth buying an ounce. You'll have to hurry with the letter but see if you can make it. I'm having a ball and feeling good to be close to home.

See you for Christmas.
Love, Jeffishna

**29 OCT 1975**

*I spent most of the day sitting around waiting for people at consulates, travel agents, banks etc. I finally bought an air ticket to Kathmandu and arranged and picked up my visa. I went back to the old town and picked up some jewellery. I had a smoke on the bus and got the super munchies in a Chinese restaurant and racked up a super bill (about 6½ dollars).*

**30 OCT 1975**

*I booked into the travel agent's hotel for the night. I just hung about all day. I watched a chess game at a park with ancient rules and four guys playing at once. I found a snooker saloon and played a few games. I also went to a shitty supermarket – I saw a chick holding a kid up to piss in the foyer. I met up with some others from the bus and we visited a very sick Don in a hospital that was not much better than in Kabul.*

Don was from Sydney and a fellow passenger on our Magic Bus from Istanbul. He fell seriously ill in Delhi and was hospitalised. Although the hospital looked significantly better equipped than the one in Kabul, and several degrees cleaner, it was very crowded: there were patients in beds lining the corridors. Even so, we were satisfied Don was in capable hands.

**31 OCT 1975**

*I was up at a ridiculous hour for a tour bus to Agra. A really shitty uncomfortable trip, but I saw the Taj Mahal – and I was not disappointed.*

Most impressive was the beauty of the Taj Mahal as a complete artistic statement. In my travels up to then I'd seen stunning architecture in many places, but the Taj seemed to be a beautiful and coherent whole,

*Taj Mahal, Agra, India*

possibly because of its celebrated symmetry.

Almost as impressive was the obvious absolute power of the seventeenth century Mughal Emperor Shah Jahan who marshalled the resources to build such a magnificent monument to his personal grief: a mausoleum for his favourite wife Mumtaz Mahal.

> The tour dragged on to a few other places, but I didn't know what I was seeing so it was not so interesting. After a really long day I got back to Delhi about 11PM and had a late dinner at The Cellar. Then I got a taxi to the airport to spend the night there to wait for my flight to Kathmandu.

**1 NOV 1975**

> I went through typical Indian bureaucracy at the airport, but finally got on the plane and had a fantastic 70-minute flight with free breakfast and a can of Heineken and a view of the Himalayas. We landed in Kathmandu and pulled up in about 50 feet of runway. Kathmandu looks cleaner and richer than India. I got a guy from the airport to take us to his Blue Angel Hotel. I walked around town then back to the hotel and got super blown away, and then just sat on the roof and tripped out on the mountains.

**2 NOV 1975**

> I was sick all day today with a super heavy cold so nothing much happened, but I stayed in bed all day. The Thai embassy is closed for the next three days so I'm stuck in Nepal until next Tuesday. A walk through Kathmandu yesterday was pretty good with an area full of temples on their last legs, and huge drums and a bell up in a tower. There are still dirty parts, but it's not half as

*crowded as India – and a nicer atmosphere.*

**3 NOV 1975**

*I went to American Express to meet Phil, but he wasn't there. On my way back I bought 'Quotations from Chairman Mao'...*

Chairman Mao Zedong of the Peoples Republic of China was a hero to the New Left political movements of the 1960s and 1970s. His 'Quotations from Chairman Mao Tsetung', commonly known as 'The Little Red Book', was a desirable acquisition – perhaps a token rebellious act.

After Mao's death in 1976 attitudes changed markedly when it was revealed his 'Cultural Revolution' of the previous decade had precipitated multiple horrors within China including famine, political purges, and ethnic persecutions with the consequent deaths of millions of people.

*...and a face mask*

Nepal's famous traditional and highly decorative face masks represented gods or demons. They were made from a variety of materials including wood or bejewelled metal. But I bought the cheaper papier-mâché masks.

*I checked out a mountain trip at the tourist office. Then went back to the hotel and got blown away before going to my third restaurant in Kathmandu and had dinner, then I went back to the hotel and crashed.*

**4 NOV 1975**

*I went back to American Express but there was still no one there. I'm getting pretty tired of the filth in this part of Asia. And I'm sick as a dog still. I weighed myself yesterday – 8 ½ stone! I've lost a stone since Istanbul (about half a pound a day). I had a Chinese dinner at a good restaurant then went* back to the hotel and crashed.

**5 NOV 1975**

I took a 40 paisa bus ride up to Patan. Not much there – Durbar Square is full of temples. The same dirty old sections. I got the bus back and went looking for another mask. I bought ink prints and met up with Phil and Jenny from the Blue Angel. We had lunch, then went back to the hotel and got blown away. I was still blown away and went and met Phil and Swede and had dinner then back to bed.

**6 NOV 1975**

I got my arse into gear and booked out of the hotel and down to the Thai embassy for a visa. Then we got a minibus to Bhandar and then climbed along trails for nine miles in four hours to Everest Lodge at 7100 feet.

"We" here being Dave, Wayne, and me. We were similarly aged Australians from the Magic Bus. We loosely travelled together after leaving the bus in Delhi. As some previous diary entries already make apparent, pairings and groups met, formed, split, and re-met along the way; it depended on whether plans and interests coincided.

We're on a mountain top with the Khat Valley on one side and a narrow valley on the other side leading to Everest – with the Himalayas along the horizon. We are the only people at the Lodge which is too expensive. Sunset had red snow on the mountains but there was too much cloud to see the peak. Had a rice dinner and crashed out.

**7 NOV 1975**

We got up too late for the sunrise. A lot of cloud again anyway. Kathmandu Valley was under fog. We had breakfast and wandered around the hilltop all morning. Later we went down to the cottage for lunch. We had an afternoon joint back on the hilltop and watched the sunset. The Himalayas are very

# Nepal

> impressive when you sit at 7000 feet and look up into the clouds and, occasionally, they would part to show mountains three times higher.

**8 NOV 1975**

> We were up early for the sunrise but there were too many clouds again, but it was still nice. We had porridge then headed down the mountain. It only took 2½ hours to get back downhill. We hopped a bus back to Blue Angel Hotel. We met some guys who told us about the Pleasure Rooms.

The Pleasure Rooms was a café-style place where people would sprawl across floor-cushions around the perimeter of a large room while chillums of hash were passed around; waiters would serve tea and sweet treats. If you finished a chillum, you would re-pack it and pass it on. It was rumoured some people spent successive days in there.

We thought it was all good fun, but there was a darker side: some on the Trail had succumbed to the drugs to their detriment; we'd seen a few causalities in Afghanistan too. We were warned to avoid these desperadoes; they would approach with a dodgy deal or nefariously try to entice you to some dubious place. Often, apparently, they had sold their passports and become stranded; many funded their next drugged oblivion by ripping off vulnerable travellers. There were stories of some embassies declining to provide consular assistance to their wayward citizens; we were especially suspicious of bedraggled and spaced-out French guys.

> We had lunch and went to the Rooms and smoked and ate cakes and toffees. I got very stoned. We wandered town with Renae and Paul then crashed back at Angel later.

**9 NOV 1975**

> A rest day. I wandered down to a coffee house for breakfast then through the markets and bought a few prints then back to the hotel and laid around the roof and read books and magazines in the sun. I did some washing and went out for dinner then back to bed.

**10 NOV 1975**

> We hired pushbikes and rode down to pick up our visas. Then went back to Royal Nepal Airlines and booked tickets to Bangkok. We rode out to a water garden and saw huge catfish. It was nice riding around town. I left the guys and rode a bit more down some back streets. Then I left the bike and met the guys again and we went back to the roof and got blown away. We went and ate banana fritters. We later met back at a silver shop then waited for hours then out to the airport to sleep in the street.

**11 NOV 1975**

> We got the flight okay – two Swedes joined us. Another good flight with breakfast and beer. We landed in Bangkok feeling really good – back in civilisation.

The transition from archaic Nepal to modern Thailand was several degrees more marked than when we crossed from Afghanistan into Pakistan: the Thai buildings were more modern; there were neon billboards; and the streets were wide and bustling with motor bikes, cars, and buses.

> Really hot and humid like the Pacific – I had all sorts of nostalgic sensations of Tahiti. A long taxi ride to the Malaysia Hotel and a bit of luxury – with a swimming pool and radio. The Swedes and Wayne got drunk and brought some chicks back. I phoned home and hung around the bar with Dave and met a few Yanks.

**12 NOV 1975**

> I checked out the embassies and travel bureaus looking for a way home – all very difficult. The Indonesian Embassy was no help either. Also checked for a letter from home. I got back to the hotel without achieving much at all. We went out on the town, got blown away first then went to a nightclub street and did a pub crawl. We all got pretty drunk, and we all got

girls and took them back to the hotel. We had a bit of an orgy then flaked out and sent them home.

**13 NOV 1975**

I went into the tourist bureau to get some info. I found a student office which had a fare from Jakarta to Perth – it looks the best offer yet. I did a bit of wandering around. Really exciting streets. The food stalls are great – all types of weird foods, clean and cheap. Still no letter or money. I got back and had dinner. The chicks turned up and I sent mine away, then went to a Bronson movie 'Streetfighter'. Then I stopped off for a beer at a club then went home. The chicks didn't turn up again.

**14 NOV 1975**

I went to the Grand Palace and Wat Pho monastery. Really fabulous architecture – the best yet. Also, really fantastic statues. The mythical figures are incredible. I bought a couple of temple rubbings at the monastery.

*The Grand Palace, Bangkok, Thailand*

The temple rubbings were made by novice monks who would hold a sheet of rice paper over the intricate stone carvings on the temple walls. Coloured chalks were then rubbed over the paper producing a print of the wall carving.

I went back to American Express and ate all the goodies on the street stalls – great food. I had dinner in the street from the back of a van. I bought a cheap Mekhong whiskey and sat in a bar with George, then we had a smoke and went on to

> the Grace Hotel. We got really bombed. Gorgeous chicks everywhere, but not there for us. I freaked out with a mirror.

Although we could live relatively well in Bangkok, we certainly weren't high-end tourists. George, who was visiting Thailand from Sydney, looked respectable but I looked like others that had travelled overland: I was wearing cheap central Asian clothes and jewellery and I had unkempt shoulder-length hair.

The nightclub bar at the Grace Hotel had full length mirrors on the walls. I was always a little self-conscious of my dress and appearance at the Grace Hotel.

That night I was relieved to see a young guy across the room; he was at least as untidy as me; then I realised I was looking into a mirror; I freaked out.

**15 NOV 1975**

> I went in to American Express and found out my money is there, but I can't touch it until Monday. I checked the post office again for a letter then walked back through jewellery shops and a ritzy suburb with jungle gardens. I got back to the hotel and hung around reading and eating burgers. We went to the Blue Fox for dinner then just hung around. We met George later and had a few joints of smack with Buddha stick.

Buddha sticks were a Thai variety of marijuana. They were widely available at a generally standard price, and conveniently packaged: several strong cannabis flower heads were wrapped around a thin 15cm bamboo splint and fastened with hemp string.

> It was very nice at the Blue Fox.

**16 NOV 1975**

> I got up, checked out, and booked the bus to Chiang Mai, then went up to see George. We got blown away and went to the railway station looking for pool rooms. We found tenpin bowling instead. We had a really good time playing a couple of games for Buddha sticks, then back to the Malaysia Hotel to get right out of it with a super double ended joint. Then over

to the Blue Fox for music and food. We got back at 7:30PM for the overnight bus to Chiang Mai. We had the only non-reclining seats – I was really pissed off and slept on the floor.

**17 NOV 1975**

Arrived Chiang Mai about 6AM. We were taken from the bus station to B&M Guesthouse – a nice new place. We had breakfast and checked out the nice little country town. I went to a market and bought a couple of shirts, then walked back to the tourist shops for silver and woodwork, but prices were a rip-off. Back at the hotel for a smoke then out on the town for dinner and a walk around then back to a coffee club with great local folk music then back to bed with a blast.

**18 NOV 1975**

I headed to Thai Silk Village to spend a fortune but ridiculous prices and didn't buy a thing. A nice bus ride out through the jungle. Back to town and played some tenpins, then walked a bit, then a taxi to another market – all closed. Checked out some silver on the way back. After dinner I did a weird score with a rickshaw driver then got stoned and went out to see the Light Festival. It was fabulous with candle boats floating down the river. Also skyrockets and Roman candles.

**19 NOV 1975**

Got up and we blew some smack to start the day. Booked out at 12AM and headed for the bus office. There were no seats left so, after getting all tense and arguing with the woman, we booked another bus. We met Wayne back at breakfast then we went on a shopping spree. I went crazy and bought lots of stuff. I saw some magnificent and cheap teak wood carvings and furniture. We went back to the room to get stoned again and then back to town for more tenpins. Then 9PM I got on a luxury liner type bus and cruised on down to Bangkok.

**20 NOV 1975**

> Back into the Malaysia Hotel and I spent the morning hassling around agencies looking for a route home, but no good. No information anywhere and Indonesia is looking really hard to get into. I decide finally to get to Penang and sort it out from there. There's no way to get there tomorrow so I got blasted and felt better. I had a bath then to the Blue Fox and I ate three hamburgers. I then hit my bed and George came in, so we had a nightcap joint.

**21 NOV 1975**

> We woke up and George came in and we got ripped. I found out that smack ain't what I thought it was! I got very stoned and went to the bank to get cheques. Hassles again and I spent the afternoon and 30 baht tearing all over town for a money changer. Back at the hotel and we had hamburgers, then we hit the Grace Hotel. I brought a chick back for a weird night – speedy. I had a swim in the pool at 4:30AM.

## My 'smack' surprise

While on my adventure, with my penchant for party drugs, I was open to experimenting with anything that might come my way. But I had one caveat: my indirect knowledge of heroin convinced me it was strictly out-of-bounds.

By that November, when I arrived in Thailand, I'd already overindulged in a few recreational drugs (marijuana, hash, and opium), which were readily procurable in the countries I had visited. In Bangkok I shared a room at the Malaysia Hotel with Dave and Wayne. They were similar-aged Australians and fellow ex-passengers off the Magic Bus from Istanbul.

We met George at the Malaysia Hotel. He was a couple of years older than us, groomed much sharper, and a proud self-proclaimed Sydney drug dealer. George was in Bangkok to buy 'smack' to take back to Sydney and had already obtained a supply which he described as pure and the highest quality. He told us it was not what you would expect to purchase as a punter in Sydney; a drug deal there would have been diluted by being 'cut' with something. George was happy to share his smack with us; I think he enjoyed our company as we explored the sensual attractions of Bangkok – he may have also enjoyed educating us about the delights of his merchandise.

We smoked the smack after sprinkling it onto multi-papered joints of Buddha sticks. Popular culture often describes the stuporous catatonic effect of heroin, but we experienced the opposite. I don't know why; perhaps it was the purity of the stuff we were enjoying, perhaps smoking rather than injecting, or maybe the Buddha stick combination. Regardless, we were off at a break-neck pace. We raced around Bangkok craving stimulation. Our favourite entertainment was tenpin bowling. We had no idea of the complexities of the game but the sensation of the rumbling heavy ball crashing into the pins was spectacular. The only ill effect of our smack experiences was aching legs the next day from striding out long distances all over town.

Two days before I left Bangkok for Malaysia, we were idly chatting in a hotel room after sharing a smack-laced Buddha joint when somebody made the semantic link between smack and heroin. I was perplexed; then not happy; then a bit anxious. I'd been smoking it for six days and, according to my ill-informed logic, I was now hooked – an addict, a junkie!

But I didn't experience any irresistible urges and, a few days later, I travelled on to Penang where I experimented with opium in a backyard den at Teluk Bahang – and the opium *did* have an appreciable stuporous catatonic effect. Maybe I was lucky that any residual heroin-honed edges I might have acquired in Bangkok were blunted by my subsequent encounter with opium.

**22 NOV 1975**

> I had an hour's sleep and was just getting horny again when Wayne burst in, so I gave up in dismay and sent the chick home. She was a real bummer – she ripped off 140 baht from my wallet. As I was packing to leave, I found a bag of grass in the top flap of my pack. I'd carried it from Herat!

I was very fortunate here. I'd carried a bag of cannabis across several borders and through a few airports. If it had been discovered there may have been awful consequences.

> I got some sleep after booking the train to Penang, then I had

a farewell smoke with George and headed out for a long night of on-and-off sleep on the train seat. The train was nicer than I expected. I had dinner on board while we rolled past flooded jungle with lit-up homes scattered through. I saw people in the jungle watching TV.

**23 NOV 1975**

I ate a decent breakfast on the train while looking around at nice jungle with huge rock outcrops sticking straight out of the plains and covered with palms and tropical plants. Also, some village temples which are huge. No real trouble at the border and I got into Butterworth at 6PM. Just a hundred yards walk onto the ferry, then I was in Penang in a few minutes. I got a rickshaw to an overpriced hotel but was too tired to move – it will do for the night. Had my best meal for long time – roast pork.

**24 NOV 1975**

I changed hotels and met up with Dave again. Then I started the hassling all over again trying to get home. I was really getting shat off. I ducked into a bar to think about it and got drunk with an RAAF guy.

The Royal Australian Air Force had a base at Butterworth since 1957; it closed in 1988.

I went out half pissed and sorted everything out, then went back to the bar to celebrate. I got home about 11PM after dinner, and as pissed as a fart.

**25 NOV 1975**

I went with Dave to recheck at the embassy before buying my tickets. It was all screwed up again. I need $200 in traveller's cheques after buying my ticket. Dave can't do it, I can – just.

## Malaysia

To qualify for an Indonesian visa, you needed to show a pre-paid ticket into and out of the country, and demonstrate access to a minimum USD200 during your stay.

> *I nearly went for Kuala Lumpur and a flight home but then changed my mind. I hassled around for most of the day with the ticket and visa. They really make you commit yourself.*

I could buy a reasonably priced ferry ticket from Georgetown in Penang to Medan in Sumatra but then I needed to navigate out of Indonesia from somewhere near my intended final destination of Bali and towards home. The cheapest option I could find was a flight to Darwin from Denpasar in Bali with a stopover via Dili in Timor.

After buying those tickets, I had just over USD200 left in traveller's cheques to satisfy the Indonesian visa requirements. My exit plan was to get to Darwin from Bali then hitchhike home to Perth from there.

> *We went down to meet Wayne at the ferry – he didn't arrive, but we met a real cool cabdriver. I went back and bought a shirt from his friend's shop.*

**26 NOV 1975**

> *I went up to Penang Hill. On the way I went through a nice suburban area. The funicular railway goes straight up the hill at 1.93:1. It's more frightening than enjoyable. It was real nice jungle though. I saw a monkey. Not much on the hill but a good view. I got back down, and Dave left about 4PM for Kuala Lumpur. No room for me at the hotel tonight so I had to move. I had a hassle at the first place then met a cool rickshaw driver*

who took me to a place. I bought a book. I'm alone again but independent too.

### 26/11/1975
**Postcard from Penang, Malaysia**

Hi,

getting from here to Australia via Indonesia is the most difficult part of the trip so far. I only just qualified for an Indonesian visa and was tempted to skip it altogether. But I decided to keep going which means I probably won't get home for Christmas. I'll probably be in Darwin then.

I got the money in Bangkok okay — ta. But I didn't get the letter, so I am just picking up small presents on the way. Some real dumb stuff with some nice stuff too. The shopping in this part of the world is fantastic. I'll have to come back here one day with a couple of grand to spare. I'm heading over to the other side of the island tomorrow to pick up a bit of tropic isle type living. Palm trees and coral coves and the like — coconuts and paw paws for lunch.

See you for New Year,

Jeff (best price),

PS: save me some Chrissie cake.

### 27 NOV 1975

I picked up everything at the embassy and bought a ferry ticket for Medan, then went over to the bus stop and got a bus to Teluk Bahang in the north of the island. I met a funny

> old lady on the bus who talked <u>at</u> me all the way. I also met some Canadians and Aussies. We got off the bus and the little old lady gets us a room for $1.50. Two chicks join us, Pam and Jane. It's a nice set-up on the beach in a fishing shack. An Aussie guy, Kevin, walks in and lights up. Later I went next door to a little old guy's opium den. A big butterfly on his singlet. I got blown away and sat up half the night talking shit with Pam.

A little skinny old man, of Chinese ethnicity, sold and dispensed opium in his small den just a few shacks away from the one we were staying in. He wore a singlet with a large butterfly print across his middle. The opium smoking was quite formal and ritualistic. The customer would lie down on their back, resting their head on a padded brick, while the old guy would load some opium paste onto a ceramic bulb at the end of a long bamboo pipe. He would apply a flame to the paste so it bubbled, and the customer would slowly inhale the vapour. For me the effect was a quiet euphoria which lasted several pleasant hours.

**28 NOV 1975**

> There's supposed to be a raid today so we're out of the house by 10AM. I went up to a waterfall with Gary (a friend of a guy I met yesterday while sitting on the beach contemplating the ocean). We met Pam and Jane on the way. Gary wanted us to have a hippie orgy in a rock pool. We went back to the beach and talked ourselves out of going in for a swim. I went for a walk around the point with Pam. We talked some more and saw some weird fish with legs. Back at the house Pam put her legs over mine and I should do something but won't (I like Pam but prefer Jane). I went and had an interesting lunch at a roundabout, then to the house and I rolled a king joint for Kevin and me, then we went and ate some more. Back at the house again I hammocked around while the others learnt Mahjong. I went to bed and read. At 12:30AM, with the light still

on and I'm sound asleep, when the cops kicked the door in. Five of them in the room, already through my pack and onto the body search. Machine guns and torches. A weird experience, half asleep and half stoned, and I could only watch — but they didn't find my stash hidden in my boot!

## 29 NOV 1975

I just hung around all day getting stoned, eating pancakes, and flying kites on the beach with the kids. I took a bike ride through town while stoned. On the way back, sometime during the day, I heard Led Zeppelin on a PA system being used for a party. The others got into Mah-jong. I got into a hammock.

## 30 NOV 1975

Same type of day again flying kites and getting stoned and hanging around in the hammock. I left about 1PM after buying three hammocks.

The hand-woven hammocks were made of colourful fibrous plastic cord; when rolled up they were very compact and light.

I caught the bus back into Georgetown then a trishaw to the wharf. I wandered onto the ferry boat at 2PM and we left. I could have easily missed it — very lucky. The boat was small but comfortable. They fed us super-chilli-hot food. I met a guy on the boat, and we blew a joint. I stood up of on the front and watched the bow wave in the sunset, and then I hit the sack rolled up in my sleeping bag on the deck.

## 1 DEC 1975

We pulled into Medan about 7AM. It took hours to get off the boat, then a bunch of us went to the bank, then I got a bus with Steve and Heidi to Parapat. It took six hours. A deadly ride with bad driving. It stopped in a town 45 km from Lake Toba. We spent two hours ballsing around in a restaurant and picking up stuff for the bus. I had fun with the kids there. We

> got into Parapat about 7PM and stayed at a Pudding Shop type place.

Parapat was the village where the ferry left for Samosir Island in the middle of the caldera Lake Toba: a favoured destination on the Hippie Trail. It was famous for the beautiful lake, lush mountainous scenery, and its laid-back people. While waiting en route at the restaurant I played peak-a-boo with some delightful kids; they were intrigued, cheeky and laughing.

My Pudding Shop comparison was because the Parapat place served the same purpose as the famed shop in Istanbul: a staging post on the Hippie Trail, though its services were more modest.

> I scored off 'Mum' who was selling by the kilo. I got stoned of course.

**2 DEC 1975**

> I got the 10AM ferry across the lake to Tuk Tuk and environs. I met up with all the people off the Medan ferry again. Toba is a beautiful lake, and the island is nicer close-up. A lot of hassles with the ferry captain and hotel owners about where to dock. We got off eventually after choosing one and took a 2km hike through paddy fields to a hotel in Ambarita. I set up the hammocks, had a delicious fruit salad, and got stoned. I stayed stoned until dinner time.

It was generous to describe our accommodation in Ambarita as a hotel. It was more of a collection of rough, thin-walled shacks with some simple spaces petitioned off to create individual rooms. The shacks were arranged around a cleared grass and dirt floored common space interspersed with tropical trees and vegetation. The restaurant was a separate shack and served excellent simple meals usually based on rice and fruit. Our hosts were delightfully friendly and keen to ensure we enjoyed our stay.

**3 DEC 1975**

> I got up and transferred from my bed to a hammock. I stayed stoned all day and only left the hammock to go to the restaurant or play frisbee. I ate a lot of food – everything just

gets written on the bill. I played a few games of chess while stoned – it was interesting, I got very involved. A nice little place to stay – garden, hammock under shelter, mountains, lake.

**4 DEC 1975**

Same as yesterday except I made a bong with the other Aussie guys and got really out of it.

A bong is a simple water pipe for deeply inhaling a small bowl of marijuana; the smoke is cooled as it passes through the water and coarse particles are filtered out.

I played frisbee and ate a lot of food, listened to music, chased pigs, hung in the hammock. I started to read 'Wuthering Heights'. The bong is really good. I played more chess and I'm learning to concentrate while stoned.

**5 DEC 1975**

I left Ambarita after bonging the last of the grass and went into Parapat to wait for the bus to Padang. While waiting I bought some more grass and Steve and I hired canoes to paddle on the lake. We had a lot of fun playing boats and pulled into little islands and blew a few joints and had a swim. The bus didn't come so we stayed for free at the hotel and blew a few more.

**6 DEC 1975**

We hired canoes again in the morning then got the bus in the afternoon to Padang. A very uncomfortable bus ride – very cramped. Nice jungle but I didn't see much out of the tiny windows. I slept on-and-off, we stopped for dinner somewhere and had a smoke which helped a bit – it was a lousy ride.

**7 DEC 1975**

We got into Padang to find out there's no Mercedes bus to Jakarta – just locals. So I got a refund – I don't fancy four days on a worse bus.

The larger Mercedes buses were primarily for longer trips and were considerably more comfortable than the smaller local-route buses.

> I decide to check out the ferry situation tomorrow. I booked into a hotel and got stoned. A lot of chess players at the hotel but I'm not in the mood. I went and saw a bad French movie. Smoked and played a word game till 1AM.

**8 DEC 1975**
> I got up and Steve had gone to the Post Office, so I checked out the Kalimantan ferry. It leaves in 1½ hours with a stop in Jakarta. We raced around and got a bus out in time only to wait for three more hours for the ferry. I saved a bit of money by taking this ferry. We smuggled the dope on board, and we met an Aussie passenger — Greg from Perth. We claimed a piece of deck and got blown away and we missed dinner. But a nice start to the boat trip — a very Sumatran scene — fishing boats, mountains, clouds, jungle etc.

**9 DEC 1975**
> Early to bed and very early to rise on the boat. I met an Indonesian guy who speaks excellent English from teaching himself out of Reader's Digests. I played good chess players and did the occasional bit of joint rolling — the other passengers don't seem to mind. Two meals a day 8AM and 4PM. A pump in a locker room is the shower and bathroom. The sea is getting a bit rough. There's not much to do but lay around.

**10 DEC 1975**
> Same schedule only I managed to fix my wine bag, so I don't have to scramble to the back of the boat anymore with a cheese tin for a drink.

My "wine bag" was a bota bag: a traditional leather wine bag. I'd carried it from Spain, and I repaired a small hole in it. Having the bag operable meant I didn't need to retrieve water in an empty cheese tin from the barrel that was stowed at the stern of the boat; I'd staked out my sitting spot at the bow.

*The highlight of the day was passing Krakatoa.*

I discovered later this "highlight" was Anak Krakatau ('child of Krakatoa' in Indonesian). The original volcanic island of Krakatoa disappeared in a cataclysmic eruption in 1883.

*We got into Jakarta about 10PM but can't dock till morning. So we rolled another one or two.*

**11 DEC 1975**

*We jumped off the boat and grabbed a bus into town. I knew my way around a bit with a rough map I'd picked up somewhere. The train station was closed so we booked Steve into a hostel, he's staying. I went to the Australian Embassy to do my bit for Gough by voting in the federal election. I spent an hour reading newspapers and listening to broad Aussie accents. On the way back I dropped into an insane department store with Christmas carols. I found a supermarket where I bought food for the train then went back to the station and arranged my ticket to Jogjakarta. I got blown away one more time with Steve and then we went to another department store. I got lost but we met up again at the hostel. I walked to the station and blew a number. Farewells all round then I boarded a disgusting third-class train for a very uncomfortable all-night ride – super cramped and hot.*

**12 DEC 1975**

*Into Jogjakarta about 7AM. I found a hotel and got washed up and went to see the town. Not much to do here but shop and that's a bit expensive. I haggled in the markets and bought some batiks and argued a couple of times with a chick about the price of a pocket calculator. I checked out some leather* jackets too. I went back to my room for a rest in the afternoon and then out on the town at 6PM. Everything comes to life. People are selling everywhere. I bought a bracelet and shirt. Had a lot of fun today hassling everyone in the shops – it's supposed to be fixed price.

**Diary Note:**
Shopping in Asia:
"Do you sell maps here?"
– "I don't know"
"How much are the melons?"
– "Why?"
"Can I have a pack of Wills Virginia, please?"
– "No"

**13 DEC 1975**

Up at 9AM and had to catch the train at 11AM, and do all my shopping, and get money, and get packed first. I ran around and did nothing. I got to the station and missed out on a seat on the train. I checked-in my pack at left luggage and went back to the shopping. I did everything and even got a handbag for nothing. I got a student discount on my train ticket and sat in the buffet learning to use my new calculator while waiting for the train. A pleasant ride to Surabaya, then a change of train for Banyuwangi. I slept on-and-off, and met two American chicks from the Peace Corps. I had good meal on the train. I'm getting excited closer to home.

**14 DEC 1975**

A connecting bus to the ferry then I crossed into Bali. I picked a losmen out of the bunch of hawkers at the jetty and moved out to Kuta.

Balinese guesthouses were called losmens. Kuta Beach was the main destination for us younger travellers. There was a triangle of adjacent localities in that area of Bali: Kuta – where we stayed; Denpasar – the main town; and Sanur – for the wealthy tourists. If the latter-day tourist meccas of Seminyak, Legian, or Cangu even existed then as villages, we were unaware of them.

> I met Kevin again from Penang.

Kevin was a tall amiable surfer from Canberra. He had a mop of curly blond hair and a laid-back grin that accorded with his manner. We had shared a few days in Penang as well as a mutual enjoyment of marijuana; what he liked to call 'hootch'. He also survived the immigration police raid we experienced in the village shacks of Teluk Bahang near Penang.

I received a short letter from Kevin in March the following year. He thought being back in Australia was "a bummer". He'd returned to the Public Service to earn some money ("I reckon it's all bullshit but it's the only place you can get some money"). He also wrote of his intentions to resign his job in the next month and head down the coast to surf; I didn't hear from him again.

> The atmosphere here is very touristy. It's not as nice as I was expecting. It's hardly as peaceful as Lake Toba or others.

Of course, Kuta in 1975, and Bali more generally, was not at all touristy compared to today; it was only marginally more than a fishing village. The losmens were typically family run collections of very modest ground-level rooms, usually detached, and with a communal ceramic-tiled porch. Our losmen had a shared outdoor 'bathroom' in the courtyard: it was a small plastic bucket under an elevated water tank tap.

Poppies Garden Restaurant was the only sophisticated restaurant in Kuta and, in today's terms, might not have warranted that description. More ordinary dining was from street vendors or open-fronted cafes. Most of the 'streets' were just palm-lined dirt laneways; temples were the only buildings higher than a single story.

My diary description of Kuta as "very touristy" probably says more about Lake Toba; most likely I was noticing Kuta's relative profusion of retail vendors catering for tourists.

> There's no sun either! I had a blue meanie soup at Junior's Café and had a very nice time listening to frogs at the swamp and then back at Mama's Restaurant with some tripping English guys.

'Blue Meanie' was the colloquial name given to a type of psilocybin mushroom. Junior's Café stood alone on a dirt track just down from central Kuta and towards the beach; it was famous for serving Blue Meanie soups and omelettes.

We were told a story about a holidaying family of dad, mum, and their two pre-teen kids who ordered a lunch of mushroom omelettes. Junior was only momentarily perplexed, and then assumed these customers must have been aware of his universal fame: he served up his mind-bending specialty.

**15 DEC 1975**

> I had a shitty morning out at Sanur trying to salvage something from the Darwin flight.

On 7th December the Indonesian military invaded East Timor. My Indonesian exit flight ticket was Denpasar – Dili (East Timor) – Darwin. The flight was cancelled because of the hostilities.

> I didn't get very far and went back to Kuta and scored two LSD trips with Kevin. I dropped a quarter at 4:30PM. Very powerful. A fantastic initial time – feeling just so good – a great party in Poppies Restaurant. I thought it was over then I went back to the losmen, and it came on again very strong. I lost reality a few times – weird. I couldn't see a roof in the dark, so it wasn't there! Mild colour flashes, and I had to steady myself a few times. A generally memorable experience.

**16 DEC 1975**

> I felt very tired and a little spacey. I went out to Uluwatu with the crew. We hired a bemo then trekked through the villages and jungle down some cliffs to a cave. It was high tide so we couldn't get out. It looked like a reasonable left-hander – nothing spectacular.

It must have been an unusually poor surf day; Uluwatu is now a very famous Balinese surf break.

> We hung around with some locals in a cave and then to a temple with monkeys. We went back to Kuta, and I had great

## Indonesia

> fish steak meal at Poppies. I rested all arvo and had a quiet night. I bought a bottle of beer and didn't finish it.

**17 DEC 1975**

> I went into Denpasar and Sanur trying to fix up my trip home. There was good surf out near the Bali Beach Hotel. I sorted out a deal with Cathay Pacific from Jakarta to Perth for $289. I sent a telegram home for more money. I put my Afghan coat in for dry-cleaning at the hotel.

My Afghan coat was made from sheepskin (or possibly goatskin) with the long dark-brown fleece on the inside and decoratively embroidered untanned leather on the outside. Most of us on the Magic Bus bought one in Chicken Street in Kabul. They were useful in central Asia – but not so much in the tropics. The leather was dubiously cured and, by now, it was stiffening, and the fleece was falling out in tufts.

> I got back to Kuta and had a joint with some chicks, then a bowl of mushie soup at Junior's. I played pool then went to the Garden Café where I listened to a Perth guy majoring in big words. Then I went back to the losmen and smoked a few joints with some nicer people.

**18 DEC 1975**

> Can't remember much of today. It could have been 'shopping at losmen' day.

There seemed to be some set days when Balinese door-to-door salesmen would visit the losmens with a range of clothes, jewellery, wood carvings and general touristy merchandise to sell to the guests. We'd all sit around on the cool porch and haggle; tea was served.

> I bought a glass moonstone ring, chopsticks, and paintings. Then mainly I just laid around. I scored more acid off John sometime around now. I took a quarter tab and went back to the losmen and slept through it all!

**19 DEC 1975**

> I went with Kevin over to Sanur with some surfboards for a

surf. It was a hassle to get the surfboards on the bemos. We finally got there and had a surf in some great waves. I wish I was in better condition — I still had fun though. After dinner a group of us went to a Ramayana dance — it was really good!

The Ramayana Ballet is a highly stylized and dramatic dance portraying an epic Sanskrit legend. The show we watched was performed outdoors in a setting surrounded by blocks of large grey stone carvings; we sat on the ground in front of a low stepped stage.

The costumes and actors were stunning: gorgeously elaborate and intricate; with a lot of makeup, masks, and gold. Their movements were either fluidly graceful or bombastically dramatic; it depended on the character being portrayed and the narrative.

There was no dialogue, but the music made up for it; it crashed and wailed with every tragic turn in the tale.

**20 DEC 1975**

I went into Denpasar to organise getting home. There's no money yet so I can't do anything about my flight. I went back to Kuta and went for a surf — good fun. Later in the arvo Kevin scored Buddha sticks and we had a session. I was sitting in my chair wishing for another joint when a teacher chick throws half a Buddha stick into my lap because she is leaving — Wow! Christmas! We got stoneder.

**21 DEC 1975**

We went to Ubud to see a cremation ceremony. We got two bemos out with Tim, Linda, Tony, and Kevin. A very hot day and a huge crowd of tourists. A big procession down the street following huge floats with the body in it. Lots of people and flowers. It was set up in a paddock and they burnt it.

This was a spectacular event; it seemed like the whole island was there. The Balinese were completely indifferent to the large number of us who were there as spectators. The entire show seemed to be a big loose noisy celebration.

> We got back to Kuta and had an omelette at Junior's. I walked around the streets while the mushies gradually came on, then I went back with Tim and rapped with Junior till 10PM, then back at the losmen with others until 4AM.

**22 DEC 1975**

> I was up very tired and went back into Denpasar after my money. But still nothing there. I went back to Kuta and sat around till mid arvo then headed back and tried again. Still no good so I went out to Sanur to pick up my Afghani coat from the dry-cleaners and I hung around the Bali Beach Hotel. I got back to the losmen and had a few joints then hit the sack hoping all would be well tomorrow.

**23 DEC 1975**

> I went back into town again – still nothing. I went out to Sanur and cancelled my booked plane ticket. Back at Denpasar I tried to phone home – no answer. I was getting worried, so I wrote to Judy and Chris.

Judy is my older sister and Chris was her husband. Why I thought my sister could do any more than my parents is indicative of my increasing desperation; she would have been subject to the same communication difficulties as my parents. Also, in hindsight, my decision-making may not have been totally sensible given my everyday intake of illicit substances over the previous few months.

> Then I went back to Kuta to try to smoke away my troubles. I can't even get any good grass. Bali is becoming an anti-climax. I went back to the telephone exchange after a fun surf at sunset. The phone call was no good again, so I went home to bed.

## 24 DEC 1975

> I spent five and a half hours from 8AM in the telephone exchange. I finally got through to Dad and found out my money has been here all the time! Furious!

It was explained to me later that the banks in Bali could profit by withholding transferred money as long as they possibly could.

I'd spent the last week trying to get by on diminishing funds, without a confirmed exit route from Indonesia, and with my visa getting uncomfortably near to expiring. There were many frantic unproductive hours in the bank, in the telephone exchange, and rushing between travel agents.

And it was becoming apparent to some people that I might be a financial liability; the usual amiable demeanour of the local businessmen towards me was beginning to fray. It was embarrassing and unnerving, especially with my losmen hosts. So, although I was "Furious!", finally having some funds again was an immediate relief.

> I got the money, then over to Cathay Pacific and the bastard was closed. I met an English super-traveller with a motorbike who took me to the airport and back. I booked a Merpati Airlines flight Jakarta to Perth. I had dinner in unreal street markets in Denpasar. Back for a pub crawl at Sanur after looking for Mr Ambarita from Cathay Pacific, then back to Kuta and I got very stoned. I stayed up till Christmas at Poppies then went home to bed.

## 25 DEC 1975

> I had a Merry Christmas chillum in the morning with everyone in a circle. Kate made a bong and we all got very stoned. I went for a fabulous surf then had a big lunch and slept in the afternoon. I then went for a frog-leg Chrissie dinner then back at the losmen I got chillumed again, and then to Poppies for more food. We then hit the beach for a party and more chillums. I spent the night on the beach with a nice chick (Cathy) and we saw a fabulous sunrise.

Cathy was on holidays from studying social work in Sydney. She was blue-eyed and pretty with straight long blonde hair. She was travelling with her friend Anne, a vivacious brunette and the more popular of the pair.

But I was attracted to Cathy's shy smile. She wrote to me in early 1976 from Sydney; she was back at her studies with plans of doing her final practical block in Perth. She also had vague plans of finding somebody to travel India with, and I was going to stay with her in Sydney on my way to a New Zealand trip later in the year. But we never caught up with each other again – like those literary 'ships in the night'.

**26 DEC 1975**

> I went with Tim over to Sanur to book a flight with Cathay Pacific in case Merpati Airlines falls through. Tim freaked over the luxury of the Bali Beach Hotel set up. We got caught in a downpour and shared a taxi with an old couple to get out of the rain— nice people, and then back to Kuta

**Entry written across bottom of pages 26 DEC 1975 & 27 DEC 1975:**

> I generally spent the mornings hassling in town then afternoons and nights getting stoned one way or another, and going out with Cathy to dinner etc. I had a fabulous trippy mushy night somewhere here when I sat on the beach around a campfire as the "King of Fire".

**27 DEC 1975**

> I went with Cathy into immigration to get a visa extension, but they say I don't need one. We went back to a cockfight – really great. I placed a few bets with a Balinese guy we met there. I lost 220 rupiah but had a good time. It wasn't half as brutal as Spanish bullfights.

Cathy and I stumbled upon this exhilarating spectacle and were captivated. Although it seemed less brutal than bullfights it was, of course, still horribly cruel; I certainly wouldn't attend another now.

But the atmosphere was loud and frantic. The men crowding around the small arena were exciting to watch as they yelled over each other while waving around fistfuls of banknotes. And they accepted us unconditionally; they drew us into their melee, and we enjoyed it.

**28 DEC 1975**

> Went to Merpati to pay for my ticket. The price has gone up $100!! Fuck them! They have got me by the balls. I wandered around all morning trying to score any drugs. Very disturbing – I had to have a smoke or something. I ended up dropping a quarter tab of LSD at 4PM. I went out for a fabulous surf at Kuta while tripping with the sunset. Then I went back to the losmen, then out to dinner – me and Cathy, Matt, and Anne. Matt and Anne split, then we went back to the losmen, and Cathy ate a Buddha stick in a banana, then we went to a puppet show. We were having a fabulous time when an earth tremor hit.

At the time we were sitting on the grass watching the traditional Wayang shadow puppets. I have a clear recollection of the Balinese crowd gasping and rising in unison; anxiously scanning the distant dark mountains.

Cathy was a novice with drugs and, now very stoned, was leaning on me with her head against my shoulder. She looked up at me and dreamily murmured – "Did it feel to you like the ground moved then?" – "Fuck, Yeah!!"

> I freaked and dragged Cathy all over the place looking for help. We got to Poppies and met up with the crew and they settled us down – "We're on an island man, where are you going to go?" We started having a lot of laughs again – then Cathy blew apart. It was 'Hysterics at Poppies' with me trying to calm her while I started going through the roof again myself. I finally got her home to bed, and I was just relaxing when I started tripping all over again. I dropped a sleeping pill at 2PM and hit the sack about 3PM. I'm off dope from now on. I'm having flashes while writing this!

## 29 DEC 1975

I went to Sanur again and bought a Cathay Pacific ticket from Jakarta to Perth on the 1st.

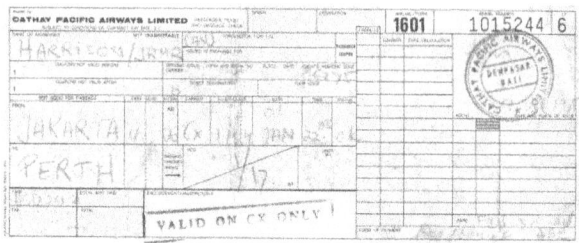

Then to immigration where they screwed me so much, I begged them to deport me. That brought on some cooperation — but it cost me $23 for three days extension. A Singapore couple before me paid $5 for ten days. I finally got something sorted then back at Kuta and I find out the buses to Jakarta are booked out. So back to Denpasar to book a Garuda flight to Jakarta — that leaves me with no money. After all this bullshit, I must go back and face Cathy. It took hours to get her talking again but, after a while, she loosened up and we had a nice night.

## 30 DEC 1975

I went back to immigration and picked up my visa (the bastards gave me ten days to cover themselves) then to Garuda to find out my flight to Jakarta has fallen through. I said goodbye to Cathy then raced around looking for a way to get to Jakarta by the 1st. At 2:30PM I found a Sempati cargo flight to Jakarta at 3:30PM. I raced back to the losmen and threw everything in my pack. I borrowed six dollars off Scott and made it to the airport. A

lousy flight – an empty plane in a thunderstorm – a real heart stopper. I got to Jakarta at 8PM in pouring rain – I fell flat on my face on a muddy footpath and into a hostel soaking wet. I crashed the night on a couch.

I was soaked through, as was my backpack. The prints, temple rubbings, and papier-mâché face masks I'd carried for weeks were all ruined.

**31 DEC 1975**

A rest day for getting cleaned up – I just laid about. Later I took an afternoon walk. Not much to see except a terrible road system – no foot paths. New Year's Eve at the hostel was fairly quiet. I bought a beer and sat around and talked. I also went to an amusement park for an hour and somebody gave me a plastic horn. Back at the hostel the owner invited me in for punch and cake and cigarettes. I hit the sack at 1AM. A nice quiet evening.

**1 JAN 1976**

I'm going home!!! Hard to believe. I met Tony and Linda again, they arrived at the hostel this morning.

# Epilogue – A Transformation

We were heading for home after they had picked me up at Perth International Airport. I was seated in the back of my dad's car, Dad driving, and Mum in the front passenger seat. They both seemed very happy to have me home at last, but also a little unsure about the changes to their only boy. Sometime later I learnt they had been out to the airport every day of the past week in anticipation of my arrival. I hadn't let them know my flight details beforehand; communicating from Indonesia was difficult, and my departure was chaotic.

I had transformed since they had last seen me nearly twelve months earlier. Initially, I suppose, my transformation was more noticeable in my appearance than my disposition. I now had shoulder length hair, formlessly shaped, and roughly brushed. Almost all my western clothes had been replaced with cheap Asian cottons; my trousers were stitched from printed flour bags. I wore an excess of low-quality jewellery: a necklace, some bracelets, and a dubious black star sapphire ring. I had lost about two stone (12.7kg) since I left Greece only fourteen weeks earlier, so I was probably a bit gaunt, and I was trying to grow a wispy moustache and goatee.

The progressive (or regressive?) changes in my appearance, up until Istanbul in September, are traced in a series of photos: the first is my Australian passport photo from 1974; the second is from late June 1975 in Amsterdam; the third is from late September 1975 in Istanbul.

From that October I went on to degenerate through three and a half weeks on the Magic Bus, followed by nearly nine and a half weeks through Southeast Asia. My parents were probably justified in their apparent perplexity; I knew myself that I was changed.

When returning home after a significant time away, after experiencing an array of adventures, it's not uncommon to be a bit dismayed with how family, friends, and your neighbourhood haven't changed with you. All seems ensconced in a time-bubble; the kaleidoscope of your experiences is not reflected anywhere. After some initial weeks of recuperative rest, and my re-acquaintance with home comforts, I began to feel as though my journey had been unreal – it was almost as if it hadn't happened. And that was depressing. I considered enlisting in the army! I don't recall where the idea began, or the flawed reasoning behind it, but I remember sitting on the lawn of my local Scarborough Beach Hotel, beer in hand in the hot Perth summer sun, and discussing my nascent plan with my friend Kim. He had 'done the overland' in the previous year and understood what I was experiencing. Thankfully, he persuaded me that, given time, I would reacclimatise. So, I forgot the urge to be a soldier and, after a brief money-saving reprise as an office worker, I enrolled at university and became a pseudo student pretending to study for my Bachelor of Arts.

But 1975 was my most educational year. I visited thirty-three countries; some only very briefly, but in others, where I spent longer, I traversed reasonably extensive regions. I learnt a lot of geography. I also broadened my knowledge of the countries I visited, and their cultures, as well as those of fellow travellers from other countries. Hours I spent in art galleries, museums, palaces, castles, churches, mosques, festivals, and theatres gave me an appreciation of the breadth of human achievement; or, sometimes, human folly. Most importantly, I was thirsty to discover more.

I learnt more about myself: how to deal with a variety of transactional and some social scenarios. I tested what I could endure, and what I might be capable of accomplishing. And I began to develop a personal set of values: what seemed important to me to live 'a well-lived life', as they say. Also, over those three hundred and forty-nine days, I met people from a wide variety of socio-cultural backgrounds; I experienced their nearly universal kindness and curiosity of their fellows. Of course, there are always a few exceptions: individuals with their own dark histories, or intent on darkening others' histories. But overwhelmingly, my encounters were positive.

I always thought I'd go back to London. I also knew I would need a valued skill to be able to earn a good living there – not just a day-to-day grind. So, life proceeded to get in the way; it took another twenty years of distraction and maturation, including some years of study, before I was appropriately qualified to return. In 1996 I surprised my justifyingly sceptical friends when I announced I was off to London. This time I was travelling on a four-year ancestry visa granted through my grandmother's English nationality, and I would be travelling with my new wife. We stayed for eight years; we holidayed frequently taking advantage of London's hub location; I revisited some places I'd been to in 1975. We could afford to travel more extravagantly than I did decades before, so they were more refined jaunts, though not necessarily more memorable – sometimes the frugal adventure, even if less comfortable, could seem more extraordinary. And, of course, life looks different through a twenty-one-year-old's prism compared to a forty-something's.

We were in Cairo on one of our holidays sometime in the late 1990s; Tracey asked our Egyptian taxi driver about the framed photo fixed onto the dashboard. He launched into an impassioned monologue describing his immense pride in his pictured daughters. He told us of his determination to work long and hard to pay for their education and secure their best futures. It was an ambition that fathers anywhere would understand, and it underlined for me what I began to believe through my year circumnavigating the globe in 1975: while our cultural differences enrich our world, our shared humanity unites us.

# GLOSSARY

I wrote my 1975 Diary, and the letters & snippets, as a twenty-one-year-old from a geographically and culturally isolated Australian city. Therefore, my then prevailing naïve 'surfie' values will reflect some of the language: some 1970s Australian, some idiomatic Perth, and some particular to my immediate group of friends.

| Term | | Description |
|---|---|---|
| a blast | : | good fun; smoke a joint |
| arse into gear | : | to get motivated |
| Aussie | : | Australian or Australia |
| ballsing around | : | ineffective or unserious activity |
| blotto | : | very drunk |
| blown away | : | amazed; drug stoned |
| bombed | : | drunk; drug stoned |
| boof | : | have sex |
| brekkie | : | breakfast |
| bugger all | : | none, nothing |
| bugger that | : | dismiss |
| bummer | : | bad experience; a pity |
| check out | : | have a look at; leave accommodation |
| chick(s) | : | girl(s); woman(women) |
| cutback | : | a surfing manoeuvre |
| deadshit | : | a person of unappealing character |
| freak | : | hippie; enthusiast (e.g., nature) |
| freak out | : | lose composure, mildly panic |
| gas | : | good (exceptionally) |
| groovy | : | fun, hip, cool |
| gutsy; gutsier | : | raw, genuine or strong; more gutsy |
| hairy | : | risky |
| hassle(d) | : | difficulty; harass; negotiate; |
| insane | : | amazing, incredible |
| mosey(ed) up | : | approach(ed) indirectly |

| | | |
|---|---|---|
| pissed; as a fart | : | drunk; very drunk |
| piss weak | : | unimpressive |
| rap | : | talk – usually intensely |
| rip | : | perform very well (a surfing term) |
| rip-off | : | over-priced; scam |
| ripped | : | stoned on marijuana |
| shat off | : | annoyed |
| shit; shit! | : | faeces (noun), rubbish (adj); damn! |
| shit-house, shitty | : | bad (exceptionally) |
| stoke(d) | : | pleased, elated |
| tea | : | the beverage; or the evening meal |
| unreal | : | see 'gas' |

# Author Bio

Jeff Harrison returned to London in 1996 as an information technology contractor after completing his Bachelor of Science.

He began his working life with government departments in Perth, Western Australia, before transferring to the far north-west Kimberley region. In later years he worked in the mining industry in the Kimberleys.

After eight years in London, he quietly retired to Byron Bay in northern New South Wales.

Most days he enjoys his garden and mucking about with oil paints in his home studio. He also enjoys a glass of wine with dinner – if it's not an allotted alcohol-free day.

www.ingramcontent.com/pod-product-compliance
Lightning Source LLC
Chambersburg PA
CBHW051535010526
44107CB00064B/2740